Purpose, Hope, and Determination

Transitioning from Ordinary to Extraordinary

by Walter R. McCollum, PhD
Foreword by André R. Lynch

Published by

McCollum Enterprises, LLC

Walter R. McCollum, PhD

Fort Washington, Maryland

ISBN 978-0-9791406-7-9

All Rights Reserved, Copyright 2016

No part of this book may be reproduced or transmitted in any form or by any means, graphic, electronic, or mechanical, including photocopying, recording, taping, or by any information storage retrieval system, without permission in writing from the publisher.

Dedication

And we know that all things work together for good to them that love God, to them who are called according to his purpose.
—Romans 8:28

Thank you, God, for providing me with wisdom to understand my lifelong purpose. Because of your guidance, I am walking in my purpose and passion. Thank you for giving me the opportunity to be a demonstration of purpose, hope, and determination. I will continue to let my light shine so that others can see your good work through me and to give you the praise and honor that you so richly deserve.

This book is dedicated to all who are impacting positive social change in the lives of others. Continue passing the mantle.

I can do all things through Christ which strengthens me.
—Philippians 4:13

Acknowledgments

To Dr. Marilyn Simon, my colleague and friend, who introduced me to the true essence of purpose, hope, and determination in higher education. I am indebted to you forever.

To the contributors of this book, thank you for your support and for all that you do to use your journey as a life-altering tactic to effect change in the world.

Special thanks to my editor, Toni Williams. Thank you so much for supporting this book project. You are phenomenal! I am very thankful for you.

Table of Contents

Acknowledgments xi
Table of Contents vii
Preface ix
Introduction 1
1 Personal Connection with Purpose 4
2 Emotional Intelligence: The Heart of Purpose 17
3 Spiritual Intelligence and Purpose: The Vertical and Horizontal Alignment 38
4 Chris Daniel, PMP 49
5 Thomas Allan Gorry, Brigadier General, USMC 62
6 Kenneth Taylor, PhD 71
7 Deborah George-Feres, PhD, PCC 83
8 Dr. Kimberly Dixon-Lawson 94
9 Dr. Pettis Perry 103
10 Annie Brown, PhD 115
11 Tom Butkiewicz, PhD 126
12 Charles Senteio, PhD, MBA, MSW 134
13 Dr. Savitri Dixon-Saxon 154
14 Dr. David Bouvin 166

15 Shana Webster-Trotman, PhD, PMP, ITIL 173
16 Jodi M. Burchell, PhD 184
17 Richard T. Brown, Jr., PhD 191
18 Saul Santiago, PhD 200
19 Terrance Campbell, MA Ed, MSISM 208
20 Walter R. McCollum, PhD 224
About the Author 239

Preface

The pursuit of excellence involves making the transition from ordinary to extraordinary. It involves the conscious choice to acknowledge, accept, and apply the necessary life tactics that will inspire others to realize that failure is never an option and invite them to step into newer realms of possibility and opportunity in local, national, and global arenas. This book outlines and provides a commentary into those tactics and extends an invitation to each of us that comes in the form of a single word—GREATER! Within each of us lies the potential to grow intellectually, spiritually, emotionally, and financially. By seizing the opportunity, we are positioned to experience greater things in life.

Readers of this book will gain an understanding of the demonstration of a specific personal mandate not just to vocalize the world change they want to see, but to put those words into tangible accomplishments that make the world a better place.

Dr. McCollum has blended the themes of purpose, hope, and determination in a way that releases a fresh breath of air for personal and professional growth and development. As an accomplished academician, mentor, and coach, he has set the stage to allow the experiences of others to enhance the lives of others. He continues to demonstrate integrity, humility, confidence, resilience, commitment, and dedication in service to others around the world. I applaud the contributions of Dr. McCollum and invite you to prepare for a life-changing experience through reading this book.

—André R. Lynch

Introduction

The hand that I was dealt consisted of the cards I needed to play and win this game called life. Each card aided in understanding the importance of purpose, hope, and determination. The extraordinary outcome is the ability to effect positive social change around the world.
—Dr. Walter McCollum

The focus of this book is to show how purpose, hope, and determination contribute to the transition from ordinary to extraordinary on the quest to impact positive change in the world. This book consists of a series of short stories from individuals who have shared their truths about their frames of reference, life experiences, struggles, and successes. Through the vast experiences of the contributors of this book, you will see how lives have been impacted and how positive social change has occurred on a large or a small scale. I also share how Emotional Intelligence and Spiritual Intelligence are important to the transition from ordinary to extraordinary. This book may inspire anyone on a quest to use his or her life to change some aspect of the world.

A focus in empirical research is searching for purpose in life or intending to accomplish something personal and meaningful that will contribute to changing something around us, whether it is our family or our community, or making a contribution to the world. My definition of purpose is having the divine assignment to perform in some way that will contribute to the greater good or to humanity. This definition includes three important components. The first component is a purpose represents an ultimate aim toward which one can make progress. The second component is that a purpose is meaningful to self. This means a person should have an interest in pursuing a purpose in life that is voluntary and self-motivating. The individual, rather than colleagues, family, or others, serves as the driving force behind the intention. Finally, and perhaps most importantly, as well as being meaningful to self, a purpose is meaningful to others who are in your sphere of influence and connected to your passion. Purpose represents an aim to act in the larger world on behalf of others or in pursuit of a larger cause. This component of the definition distinguishes purpose from meaning, which is a more internally oriented concept.

In the first chapter, I share my personal connection with purpose. The next couple of chapters include a demonstration of how Emotional Intelligence and Spiritual Intelligence are aligned to purpose. Lastly, contributors who have used their lives to effect positive social change in the world through purpose, hope, and determination will share their experiences in more than 15 short stories. These stories are from doctoral degree holders or candidates who have used their ordinary lives to make extraordinary contributions in the world.

1
Personal Connection with Purpose

The man without a purpose is like a ship without a rudder – a waif, a nothing, a no man.

— Thomas Carlyle

It is important to understand that your purpose in life is why you are doing what you are doing. It is not about what you are doing. Some people spend their life doing all kinds of things; they are doing all kinds of things but don't really know why they are doing them. Their life has become consumed with busy stuff. When you reflect on why you are doing what you are doing, you begin to examine the purpose of life. I remember when I was growing up, I would say, "My purpose is to become wealthy." However, "becoming wealthy" falls under the "doing" category. To discover what my purpose in life would become, I had to focus on why I wanted to become wealthy and exactly what becoming wealthy meant to me. For me, becoming wealthy isn't about monetary gains; it is more about how I can use my life to effect change to enrich others' lives.

We all have gifts and talents given by God (or whoever your supreme being is) that are often aligned with what we are passionate about. We were given those gifts and talents to effect change in the world. For example, I have a natural gift and passion for service that I have used to serve others in countries such as Haiti, South Africa, and Costa Rica. Another gift and passion of mine is mentoring, primarily doctoral learners. For some, this is a chore or task, but for me it comes naturally with little effort, and it's something I'm good at. I'm good at it because of my Emotional Intelligence and Spiritual Intelligence skills and competencies and my ability to connect with others both emotionally and spiritually.

Purpose should involve activity that can be measured or evaluated in some way to show the benefit, impact, or effect on the greater good based upon the attainment of your goal. For example, my passion for mentoring doctoral learners can be evaluated by the number of dissertation committees I have chaired and the number of students who have earned their doctoral degree under my mentorship and are using their scholarship and research to change the world in some way. When I started mentoring doctoral learners 10 years ago, my goal was to increase the number of male

African American doctoral degree holders in the United States. To date, I have chaired the dissertations of over 50 doctoral learners (80% have been males of color), have graduated them, and am now benefitting from witnessing how they are using their doctoral experience to impact change in the world. This is a great outcome, as some academics don't achieve this level of success in 20 years of mentoring doctoral learners.

Purpose should be memorable and specific enough to be remembered and embraced. As you are on your quest to achieve your purpose in life, remember the experiences along the way. Remember the good, the unpleasant, the successes, and the challenges. All these experiences shape us into the beings that we are. When we embrace our life experiences and use them as lessons for further growth and development, we are likely to connect to purpose in the long run. Growing up as an only child in a single-parent household in South Carolina was challenging and emotionally draining. The social plights that I experienced contributed to my connection to purpose and passion. Purpose often comes from pain. The prize you will receive from embracing your experiences is your ability to experience your transition from ordinary to extraordinary firsthand. As a result of my frame of reference and my many experiences, I continue to celebrate my ongoing growth and development, and I am grateful for the enlarged territory in which I have effected positive change in the world.

Purpose should be meaningful and should surround issues that make a difference. It doesn't matter if the issues are micro or macro, as long as they make a difference and as long as you realistically have the ability to effect change regarding the issue. As I indicated earlier, service is the gift that I am passionate about. I remember my paternal grandfather serving as an honorary deacon in his church and driving the church van to transport the senior congregants to and from church, visiting the sick in the nursing home, and playing Santa Claus and giving gifts to children in the local community. That was his way of serving his community. I have used my grandfather's model of excellence in service on a macro scale to effect change aligned to poverty in poor countries such as Haiti, Costa Rica, and the Philippines. I enlisted in the U.S. Air Force when I was only 17 years old. When I was 20 years, I was stationed in the Philippines and was introduced to extreme poverty in Angeles City, right outside Clark Air

Base. Until that time, I had thought I knew what poverty was, but I found true poverty in the Philippines. Children lived right outside the front gate of the military base in cardboard boxes and this was their only shelter. Some had no shoes and others had no clothes. I became burdened by the condition of children in poverty because I had grown up in poverty in a lower class, single-parent household. Although I didn't go without the necessities, my mother had to work two jobs to support the household. Because of my passion for service, I was eager to serve the less fortunate. First, I became engaged in the Protestant chapel on base and served in various ministries. It was through the men's ministry that I began working in local communities in the Philippines where I led food drives and clothes drives to provide children with the essentials of life. From that experience, I became involved in missions around the world to contribute to the betterment of humankind. My purpose of serving the less fortunate is meaningful and connects with a real-world issue: poverty.

Even as a child, I was passionate about serving or lending a helping hand. This passion stemmed from my upbringing in church and being involved in some type of ministry, whether it was ushering, working with the youth or homeless, or singing on the choir. I began working in summer programs at the age of 14. The summer programs were for youth classified as living in low-income households. One job involved working in a horticulture program at my high school, which gave me the opportunity to learn how to garden and cultivate produce. To help contribute to our household, I grew vegetables such as green beans and cabbages and took them home to my mother to offset the cost of food. This was service at its best at the age of 14. I also drove a school bus my junior and senior years of high school and earned almost $400 a month, which was a lot of money for a high school student in the 80s. Back then, high school students could drive school buses in South Carolina. I used the money to buy school clothes and contributed to the household.

I was fortunate and blessed to grow up with both sets of my great-grandparents, who demonstrated what it looked like to serve the family and community. During my adolescent and teen years, I spent a lot of time on a farm in South Carolina with my maternal great-grandparents. I remember my great-grandfather plowing the fields with his mule named Blue from sunup to sundown. I helped him milk the cows, gather eggs from the nests, and cut pulpwood. All this training provided me with a foundation of learning to serve the family and ultimately the community. When you are connected to your purpose, you will take it with you wherever you go.

Purpose is mobile and can travel with you no matter where you find yourself. One of the things I've realized over the past 20 years is that people around the world, regardless of their ethnicity, gender, or class, all have dreams and aspirations. Sharing your story or testimony may lead someone to a better place in life through encouragement and inspiration. In 2006, I authored a book titled *Strength of a Black Man: Destined for Self-Empowerment* to effect change among youth and men of color who were challenged by the social plights around them. Because I had experienced some of the same plights and had put strategies in place to beat the odds of not becoming a statistic, my purpose was to help support other men by sharing knowledge, tools, and resources so they could become empowered in various areas of their lives. After publishing the book, I received countless letters from incarcerated men who shared how the book impacted their lives. I also received e-mails and letters from single women who were raising boys in a single-family household and didn't know how to guide them effectively. While women are to be commended for doing the best they can in raising boys alone, there are some things that only a man can teach a boy. I was able to use the book as a means for effecting change in the lives of boys and men of color.

The fact that I'm able to serve anywhere in the world keeps me connected to my purpose and passion. I always know that I'm using my life, my experiences, and my heart to effect ongoing change, whether I'm in the Western Hemisphere or North America. We all have something to give. Truth be told, most people don't want anything from you. They just want to feel a little bit of you. That emotional or spiritual connection can change someone's life or even save a life.

Most importantly, purpose is moral. There is no question about having the capacity to do something when you know it is the right thing to do. I remember when the earthquake affected nearly three million people in Haiti. The earthquake caused major damage in Port-au-Prince, Jacmel, and other parts of the region. Many countries responded to appeals for humanitarian aid by pledging funds and dispatching rescue and medical teams, engineers, and support teams. I desperately wanted to get involved because it was the right thing to do and because I wanted to serve in some way. I partnered with a Christian organization and went to Port-au-Prince to help clear rubble so commercial establishments could be rebuilt. Over the next several years, I returned to Haiti to serve in some way. I have made a life-long commitment to Haiti to support educational and technology initiatives, mentor young men between the ages of 16 and 25 in areas of leadership and professional development, and lead education and cultural delegations. The delegations consist of doctoral learners with aspirations to conduct research in the region, work in orphanages, or work with education officials at Université Quisqueya and the Ministry of Education. When it feels right and it aligns to your purpose and passion, do it!

Over the years, I've heard people say, "I don't know what my purpose is." It is not uncommon not to know your purpose. Finding your purpose is about experiencing life, being burdened by something that is affecting the greater good, being passionate about something meaningful to you, using your gifts and talents to effect change in the world, and doing what feels right.

Discovering your life purpose is one of the most fulfilling journeys that you can take. Here are five steps that may help you arrive at that point:

1. *Your life purpose matters to you. Find that one thing that absolutely catches your interest.* Search deep into your heart and pinpoint the one thing that captivates you. What's the one thing that you'd feel fulfilled to pursue?
2. *It should serve people around you. Lend some of your time and do some volunteer work.* Your life purpose should have an impact on your community or the world in some way—it should be something that you love doing and something that people love seeing you do. After all, purpose is best when shared with others.
3. *Your life purpose should enhance your growth as a person. Pinpoint your primary gifts and talent.* Some people say they are good at everything, but that isn't true. You are good at some things and average at others. You can find out your talent if you know which of your abilities are *unique to you* and set you apart from others because you do them so well. What is the skill that compels people to

come up to you and say, "Wow, you really have a skill for that?"

4. *Passion, service, and talent should all be interrelated to form your life purpose. Connect the dots.* Once you have discovered the one thing that you love doing, the one thing that you can use to serve others, and the one thing that you're very good at, you might be surprised to find that all of these are connected.

5. *Act on it.* Your family, colleagues, or friends may discourage you and tell you to just sit back, have faith, and let things happen. *Faith without works is dead!* Move forward with intention. Serve people by doing the one thing you're passionate about. Reach out to mentors in the same industry that you're targeting. Finding out your life purpose isn't about attending classes, dissecting self-help theories, or working on a dissertation. It's about exploration—it's an adventure that you can only take if you are willing to.

Your life purpose is the reason you exist and the purpose behind you living in the now, on this planet. It's the reason the fabric of your being exists and the way you will decide if your life was worth it. It's easy to get lost in the challenges and social plights of life and lose your way. You can fall asleep at the wheel as your life becomes consumed with mundane details, or joy and meaning can begin to evaporate when things you face become difficult. Having a clear indication of your purpose keeps you motivated, focused, and able to tap into your faith when you face challenges, because you understand the why behind the events in your life.

In essence, discovering your purpose requires you to spend some time with yourself and getting to know yourself by learning your strengths, weaknesses, gifts, and talents; what you are passionate about; what has meaning to you; and growth opportunities. Some people find it difficult to discover their purpose in life because the world around them is so noisy and the constant noise precludes them from initiating the process of finding solitude or a quiet place to spend time with themselves to focus on their inner self. Discovering your purpose begins with knowing your inner self and knowing how you can become your best self to serve humankind and effect change in the world! Discovering your purpose also begins with knowing what's meaningful to you, what you're passionate about, or what you're burdened by in the world that needs changing and making an emotional connection to the change within you that propels you to impact change in the world. When you realize that Emotional Intelligence is the heart of purpose, you are well on your way to transitioning from ordinary to extraordinary!

2
Emotional Intelligence: The Heart of Purpose

We cannot tell what may happen to us in the strange medley of life. But we can decide what happens in us—how we can take it, what we do with it—and that is what really counts in the end.

—Joseph Fort Newton

Emotional Intelligence is a critical component in the process of discovering your purpose. It's like a compass consisting of self-awareness, self-control, and interpersonal relationships navigating you to your purpose. The ability to have self-regulation and effective relationships has a direct connection with people living more effective and satisfying lives. Bar-On (2010) indicated Emotional Intelligence is an integral component of positive psychology and provided a route where Emotional Intelligence can be more clearly understood as a source of greater well-being and happiness. To gain all the value that Emotional Intelligence has to offer us individually and socially requires that we look at more than simply managing destructive emotions such as anger and anxiety and start using emotions as an adaptive and healthy way to bring out our best self.

Emotional Intelligence is a person's ability to understand and use emotions for a positive purpose. A person with a high level of Emotional Intelligence is able to understand not only his or her own emotions, but also the emotional status of others around him or her and make them feel positive. This is critical when trying to impact positive change in others. Intellectual Intelligence is necessary to solve logical problems and understand the functioning of the world, but Emotional Intelligence is a prerequisite for succeeding in every aspect of life. This is evident from the fact that many gifted people with an incredibly high level of Intellectual Intelligence have been largely unsuccessful socially and professionally.

Emotional Intelligence is the entry point to the development of self-management, social awareness, relationship management, and self-awareness in an individual. It allows a person to be conscious of his or her emotions and the impact they have on others. They also have the ability to change with circumstances and to understand and react to other people's emotions. No matter what type of change we choose to impact in the world, people with emotions are involved in the process. The sooner we are able to embrace and make change within ourselves, the more we will be able to change, empower, or enrich the lives of others.

Success is determined largely by the way you handle and react to unexpected situations and not by what situations arise. People who are able to react quickly and properly to such situations and get up after every fall become emotionally connected to purpose. This is partly because after each fall, they build more of their inner self through lessons learned and they gain a greater understanding of how important it is to fall to be able to use your life as an instrument to effect change in the world.

I share my testimony when mentoring others so they can understand how many times I have fallen in life and how the lessons I've learned as a result of falling contributed to something greater than myself—effecting change in other countries through international development and shaping the scholarly identity of doctoral learners. People should know the importance of falling or even failing in life and being able to get back up and apply what they learned from the fall. I often hear people say failure is not an option. For me, failing is an option and will continue to be an option as I continue growing. The most poignant lessons I gleaned from failing propelled me closer to my purpose.

Your Emotional Intelligence gives you the ability to take everything negative, such as failing or falling, in stride. It allows you to focus on your target, despite the obstacles, and to be positive when everything seems to be going against you. In other words, optimism and resilience are the hallmarks of an emotionally intelligent person.

Emotional intelligence is a natural gift for some people, but for others, it is the product of their life experiences. For me, it's a combination of both. I consider both natural gifts and life experiences to be integral elements that lead to purpose and a nice mapping to Daniel Goleman's Emotional Intelligence model.

Below are the five components of Goleman's Emotional Intelligence model:

1. *Self-awareness.* The ability to recognize and understand your moods, emotions, and drives, as well as their effects on others.
2. *Self-regulation.* The ability to control or redirect disruptive impulses and moods; the propensity to suspend judgment to think before acting.
3. *Motivation.* A passion to work for intrinsic reasons that go beyond money or status; a propensity to pursue goals with energy and persistence.
4. *Empathy.* The ability to understand and relate to the emotional makeup of other people; the skill to treat people according to their emotional reactions.
5. *Social skill.* The ability to manage interpersonal relationships and build interpersonal networks and the ability to find common ground and build rapport with others.

When connecting to your purpose, it is advantageous to have high Emotional Intelligence and to demonstrate the characteristics from the five components of this model. For example, in my purpose of mentoring scholars internationally, I've learned that students may begin to develop their own Emotional Intelligence skills and competencies through modeling their mentor's behaviors.

The same holds true for any purpose connected to effecting positive social change. Those who embrace your purpose may begin their own journey of connecting to purpose by modeling the behavior you demonstrated in connecting to your purpose. All five components in Goleman's Emotional Intelligence model are critical ingredients that inform the way a person approaches connecting to his or her purpose and passion.

Having good Emotional Intelligence pays off, and people can use it in the process of connecting with their purpose. When you model Emotional Intelligence characteristics, you might impact change in someone else through the development of their own Emotional Intelligence skills and competencies. It's also good for you to know which of your Emotional Intelligence competencies need to be improved and how to improve them. Continual growth and development are necessary when connecting to your purpose. A few years ago, I became a certified Emotional Intelligence mentor, and as part of the certification process, I had to take the Emotional Intelligence assessment and Personality Inventory based on Goleman's Emotional Intelligence model. The results from my assessment and inventory appear in the next sections.

Emotional Intelligence Assessment Results

My score on the Emotional Intelligence assessment was analyzed and is depicted in the graphics below. My score is shown in gray, and the average score for each subscale is shown in yellow. The error bars represent an average score. If the score falls above or below the error bars, I scored high or low for that subscale, respectively. If I want to raise my Emotional Intelligence, the subscales of Emotional Intelligence on which I scored the lowest should be the focus of my development.

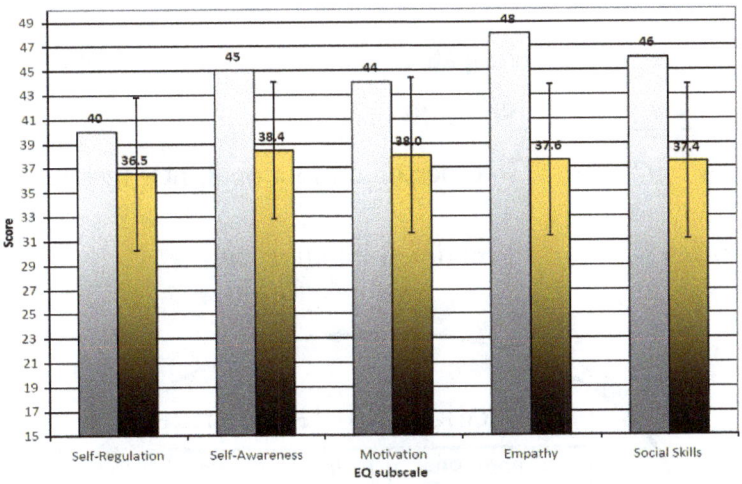

Scoring Information

The sum of the Self-Regulation, Self-Awareness, and Motivation subscales represents my Intrapersonal

Emotional Intelligence Score. The Empathy and Social Skills subscales add up to represent my Interpersonal Emotional Intelligence Score. My level of Emotional Intelligence was calculated by summing the Intrapersonal and Interpersonal Scores.

Score:	Scale:
40	Self-Regulation
45	Self-Awareness
+ 44	Motivation
129	Intrapersonal Emotional Intelligence
48	Empathy
+ 44	Social Skills
92	Interpersonal Emotional Intelligence
129 + 92 = 221	Emotional Intelligence

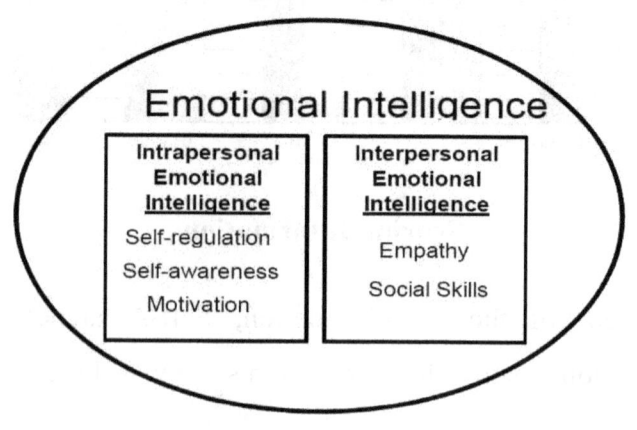

Scoring Interpretation

A higher score indicates a higher level of Emotional Intelligence. This instrument can help identify areas of relative weakness and target specific areas for improvement. The highest score for each subscale is 48. I scored a 48 on the Empathy subscale. The lowest score for each scale is 0. Because there are five subscales, the total Emotional Intelligence score is out of 240 points. My Emotional Intelligence score is 223, and I consider Emotional Intelligence one of my strengths.

Emotional Intelligence

Emotional Intelligence is the ability to sense, understand, and effectively apply the power and acumen of emotions to facilitate high levels of collaboration and productivity. An overall score indicates the level of overall Emotional Intelligence. The higher the number, the more emotionally intelligent a person is!

Intrapersonal Intelligence

Intrapersonal Intelligence is a component of Emotional Intelligence that refers to the ability turned inward. This is the ability to understand oneself. It is the capacity to form an accurate concept of oneself and to use that concept to operate effectively in life. The higher the number, the more Intrapersonal Intelligence a person has!

Self-Regulation:

Self-regulation, a component of Intrapersonal Intelligence, is the ability to control or redirect disruptive impulses and moods and the propensity to suspend judgment and think before acting. Self-regulation is characterized by trustworthiness and integrity, comfort with ambiguity, and openness to change. Although people cannot choose when to be emotional, individuals who score high on self-regulation tend to be able to choose how long that emotion lasts.

Self-Awareness:

Self-awareness, a component of Intrapersonal Intelligence, is the ability to recognize and understand one's moods, emotions, and drives, as well as their effect on others. Self-awareness is characterized by self-confidence, realistic assessment of the self, and a self-deprecating sense of humor. Persons scoring on the low end of self-awareness may find it hard to make decisions or express their emotions.

Motivation:

Motivation, a component of Intrapersonal Intelligence, is a passion to work for reasons that go beyond money or status and a propensity to pursue goals with energy and persistence. Those scoring high on motivation have a strong drive to achieve, are optimistic even in the face of failure, and have a strong sense of organizational commitment. Optimistic thinking is the key to this persistence; individuals scoring on the low end of the motivation subscale tend to have a pessimistic approach and often have thoughts along the lines of "I failed again."

Interpersonal Intelligence

Interpersonal Intelligence is the ability to understand other people. This component of Emotional Intelligence enables a person to relate effectively to other people. One who is Interpersonally Intelligent can understand what motivates others, how they work, and how to work cooperatively with them. The higher a person's score, the more Interpersonal Intelligence that person has!

Empathy:

Empathy, a component of Interpersonal Intelligence, is the ability to understand the emotional makeup of other people.

Those scoring high in empathy are able to treat people according to their emotional reactions, are expert in building and retaining talent, are sensitive to others of different cultures, and provide great service to both clients and customers. The extremes of the empathy spectrum are clearly differentiated. Those with high scores tend to experience emotion when they see someone else suffer, and as a result, they tend to be altruistic. Persons with low scores do not have strong emotions and will experience similar responses when observing both mundane and shocking events.

Social Skill:

Social skill, a component of Interpersonal Intelligence, is a proficiency in managing relationships and building networks. Those scoring high in social skill have an ability to find common ground and build rapport with others, are persuasive, are effective in leading change, and are expert in building and leading teams. Those individuals scoring low on social skills may find interactions with others awkward and difficult.

If a person scores lower than expected, there is hope; Emotional Intelligence can be learned and increased. Emotional Intelligence is independent of a person's level of general intelligence; Emotional Intelligence and IQ are two different paths to success. When a person possesses both, that person maximizes the chances for success!

Personality Inventory

My score on the personality inventory was analyzed and is depicted in the following graphics. Each personality trait exists on an inventory spectrum, with low scorers displaying opposite characteristics than high scorers. As the score is an average, individuals with average scores tend to use each pole equally or do not have a strong preference.

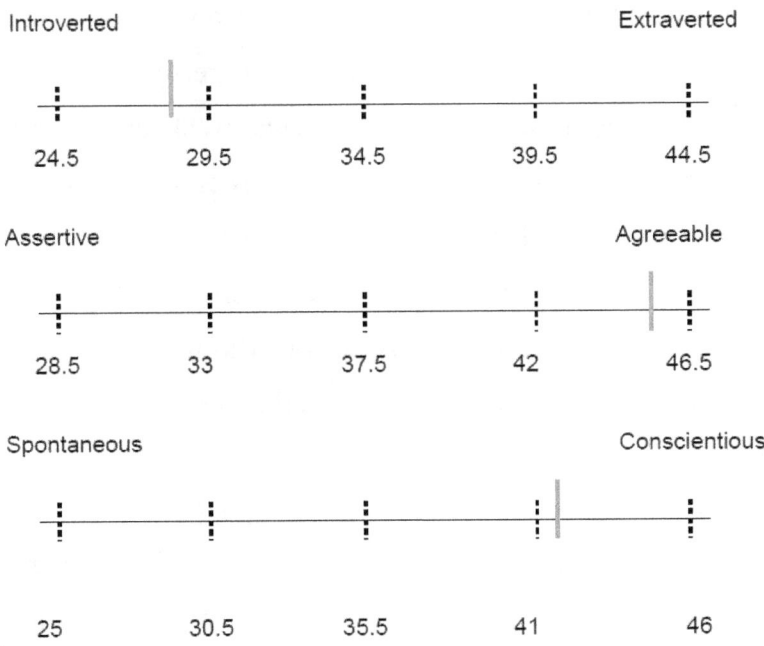

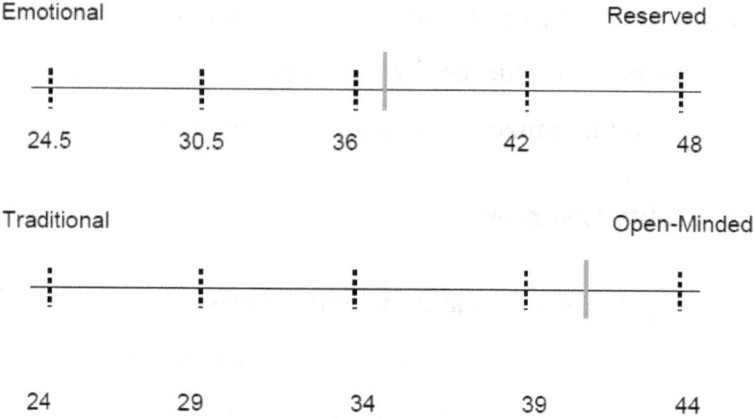

Scoring Interpretation

A person's personality is a stable disposition that remains consistent over time and across situations and that affects thoughts, emotions, and behavior. A personality scale can help raise self-awareness by giving a person a deeper understanding of his or her strengths and weaknesses based on personality type. A person's reactions and responses to stressors are based on two determinants: personality and situation. In many cases, it is an interaction of the two, with either playing a bigger role. A person who understands his or her personality can increase self-awareness and can make self-regulation easier.

The range of possible scores is from 9 to 45. The higher a person's score, the higher that person is on that particular trait. Each trait indicates a preference for behaving in a certain manner. For example, if a person scores high on extraversion, it doesn't mean that he or she can't be or act introverted; it simply means that person naturally prefers to be an extravert. If a person falls in the middle, that person tends to experience both sides of the spectrum equally. If a person scores high on introversion, it means that person naturally prefers to be an introvert.

Introvert vs. Extravert

The Extraversion subscale measures the tendency to experience positive emotions. A high score indicates the propensity to be sociable, gregarious, assertive, talkative, and active. Extraverts tend to like working in teams and tend to make natural leaders. Those scoring low on the scale are likely to be introverted: quiet, low key, and deliberate. A person who scores low on extraversion tends to experience positive emotions less frequently. This is termed introversion. Introverts would rather have their own office than work in an open environment with excessive noise. Extraverts feel energized during and after social activities, whereas introverts get their energy from ideas.

Assertive vs. Agreeable

Agreeableness measures an individual's concern with cooperation and conformity. Individuals scoring high on the Agreeableness subscale value harmony and getting along with others and are considerate, generous, helpful, compliant, tolerant, flexible, and friendly. They tend to believe that other people are good, honest, decent, and trustworthy. They also tend to be more interested in others than in themselves. Individuals scoring low on the Agreeableness subscale place their self-interests above the interests of others. Skepticism about motives leads them to be suspicious, unfriendly, and uncooperative. They are seen as argumentative and opinionated.

Spontaneous vs. Conscientious

Conscientiousness measures the way people control and regulate their impulses. Conscientiousness entails the need for achievement and dependability. Those scoring high tend to engage themselves in purposeful planning, avoid trouble, and generally achieve success. Individuals with an extremely high score on this scale may be considered perfectionists, workaholics, stuffy, or even boring. They like to have a plan for everything. Those on the lower end of the spectrum are more spontaneous. They are likely considered lazy, sloppy, or unreliable. They may be underachievers not living up to their fullest potential.

Emotional vs. Reserved

The Emotionality subscale measures a tendency to experience negative emotions. A high score is associated with a calm demeanor and freedom from persistent negative feelings. An emotionally stable individual will generally be highly optimistic and quick to rebound from stressful situations. Individuals with low scores have tendencies to be depressed, anxious, angry, embarrassed, emotional, worried, or insecure. Those scoring low have more intense emotional reactions than do most people. They may be quick to take offense or react angrily if they do not regulate these emotions properly.

Traditional vs. Open-minded

The Openness subscale distinguishes imaginative and creative people from down-to-earth and conventional people in terms of beliefs. Sometimes this subscale is termed Intellect or Culture. Those with a high score on the Openness subscale are likely to have an appreciation for art and strong intellectual curiosity and may hold unconventional and individualistic beliefs. Those high on this scale seek complexity, accept innovation, and tend to be creative. Those scoring low on this scale are likely to have narrow, common interests; be conservative; and prefer familiarity and simplicity—and they may be resistant to change.

How to Best Work With Each Personality Style

An awareness of the various personality components will not only enable a person to understand him or herself better, but will also help that person work with other people. People who receive an extreme score on a subscale have very strong preferences for their interactions and lifestyle; these preferences may or may not complement others' style. Recognizing those who tend to score either very high or very low can help with communication and teamwork. The following is a guide for how to best work with people who score on the extreme ends of the personality dimensions spectra.

EXTRAVERSION	HIGH: Extravert	Extraverts are generally talkative and easy to start a conversation with. Because they seek interaction with other people and tend to be involved in many activities, they do their best work collaboratively.
	LOW: Introvert	Introverts tend to get overwhelmed when exposed to sensory stimulation from people and social situations. They prefer to work alone and are private regarding personal matters. Note that this does not mean they are shy or lacking in social skills.
AGREEABLENESS	HIGH: Agreeable	Those individuals scoring on the extreme end of Agreeableness are friendly and easy to get along with. Their highly agreeable nature usually manifests itself as people-pleasing behavior. When they agree with you or follow your instructions, they may be doing so to avoid confrontation. Make sure they know that you welcome respectful disagreement and debate.
	LOW: Assertive	Those individuals scoring very low on the Agreeableness dimension will likely confront you quite bluntly and directly about most matters. Even though they may seem uncooperative and opinionated, you can usually take their words as constructive criticism.
CONSCIENTIOUSNESS	HIGH: Conscientious	Extremely conscientious individuals prefer rigid structure and control. You can count on them to be very dependable and achievement-oriented. They have a low tolerance for ambiguity and sloppiness. If you answer their questions incompletely or are late, they may be annoyed with you.
	LOW: Spontaneous	Those extremely low in conscientiousness are quite spontaneous and, at times, unreliable. They do not like to schedule their time and are very relaxed about handling responsibilities.
EMOTIONAL STABILITY	HIGH: Reserved	Since emotionally stable individuals tend to respond to stressful situations in a calm, steady, and secure way, they are generally easy to interact with without miscommunication. Keep in mind that this extreme group may not be as emotionally expressive.
	LOW: Emotional	Realize that those very low in emotional stability may react to stressful situations through negative thought processes, a heightened intensity of emotions, and/or exhibiting out-of-character behavior. Thus, be aware that he or she may need an extra minute or two to self-regulate, as opposed to those who do so naturally. A positive aspect of neurotics is that they tend to worry more than those who are emotionally stable, leading to great achievements and attention to detail.
OPENNESS	HIGH: Open-Minded	Persons on the extreme high end of openness tend to be unconventional and seek new ways of doing things. Since they are likely to be creative and innovative, they will do their best work when they have the freedom to pursue tasks as they see fit.
	LOW: Traditional	Persons on the extreme low end of openness prefer expert ideas and opinions as well as traditional beliefs. They prefer simplicity, so clear instructions work best.

Emotional Intelligence is a critical component in the process of connecting to your purpose. If you have good Emotional Intelligence, you will typically be successful in building and managing relationships and helping others grow and develop in their quest to develop their own Emotional Intelligence skills and competencies. When you use Emotional and Spiritual Intelligence as critical success factors for connecting to purpose, positive social change occurs. Since deploying these critical success factors, I have expanded my positive social change influence globally. I encourage you to take Goleman's Emotional Intelligence Assessment and Personality Inventory and compare your results with the averages on both the assessment and inventory to see which areas need improvement. When you know your strengths and weaknesses related to the five components of Goleman's Emotional Intelligence model, you can begin to develop your Emotional Intelligence framework, which is the nucleus to connecting to your purpose more effectively. In the next chapter, I will show how Spiritual Intelligence is aligned to purpose.

References

Bar-On, R. (2010). Emotional intelligence: An integral part of positive psychology. *South African Journal of Psychology, 40*, 54-62.

3
Spiritual Intelligence and Purpose: The Vertical and Horizontal Alignment

The knowledge of the Spirit is the true secret of creativity, leadership and happiness. It is spiritual intelligence that makes an ordinary person extraordinary. When an extraordinary person loses his spiritual intelligence, he becomes quite ordinary.

—Awdhesh Singh

Spiritual Intelligence is inherently difficult to define. It is the human capacity to ask ultimate questions about the meaning of purpose and to experience simultaneously the seamless connection between each of us and the world in which we live. According to Sisk and Torrance (2001), Spiritual Intelligence is the ability to use a multisensory approach to problem solving and to learn to listen to one's inner voice. According to Wolman (2003), each of us possesses Spiritual Intelligence, and we have the capacity to think with our souls. Zohar (2005) noted Spiritual Intelligence is an ability to access higher meanings, values, abiding purposes, and unconscious aspects of the self and to embed these meanings, values, and purposes in living a richer and more creative life. Signs of high Spiritual Intelligence include an ability to think out of the box, humility, and an access to energies that come from something beyond the ego, beyond just me and my day-to-day concerns. Spiritual Intelligence is the ultimate intelligence of the visionary leader. Spiritual Intelligence guided men and women such as Churchill, Gandhi, Nelson Mandela, Martin Luther King, Jr., and Oprah. The secret of their leadership was their ability to inspire people, to give them a sense of something worth struggling for through the connection to something larger than themselves. This same type of intelligence can be seen in those who are on the quest to connect to their purpose to change the world in some way!

But what is this "something larger than ourselves"? It is something beyond our ego-self or constricted sense of self. It may be defined as being connected to two components: the vertical and the horizontal.

- The vertical component refers to something sacred, divine, or timeless. You may think of this as a Higher Power, Source, Ultimate Consciousness.

The vertical component reflects the desire to be connected to and guided by this Source.
- The horizontal component refers to being of service to others and to the planet.

Of the aforementioned definitions of Spiritual Intelligence, the one most closely aligned to seeking purpose is the perspective of Zohar (2005), who indicated that all human beings are born with the capacity to use Intellectual Intelligence, Emotional Intelligence, and Spiritual Intelligence to some degree, because each contributes toward survival. Similar to Emotional Intelligence, the components of Spiritual Intelligence can be nurtured and developed.

When aligning Spiritual Intelligence to purpose, Zohar's 12 principles are a good place to start:

1. *Self-awareness.* This principle differs from Goleman's emotional self-awareness addressed in Chapter 1, which referred to knowing what we're feeling at any given moment. Spiritual self-awareness means to recognize what one cares about, what one lives for, and what one would die for. It means living true to oneself while respecting others.

2. *Spontaneity*. Being spontaneous does not mean merely acting on a whim. It refers to authentic behavior honed by the self-discipline, practice, and self-control of the martial artist. Being spontaneous means letting go of childhood problems, assumptions, interpretations, prejudices, and projections; being responsive to the moment; and appreciating "the power of now." And spontaneity echoes responsibility, which reminds us to use it responsibly in the moment.
3. *Holism*. In quantum physics, holism refers to systems that are so integrated that each part is defined by every other part of the system. What a person thinks, feels, and values affects the whole world. Holism encourages cooperation, because as people realize they are part of the same system as everyone else, they take responsibility for their part in it. A lack of holism encourages competition, which encourages separatism. Human enterprises need leaders who can foster cooperation and a sense of oneness to be more effective.
4. *Being vision- and value-led*. Vision is the capacity to see something that inspires us; it means something broader than a company vision or a

vision for educational development. It seeks answers to the bigger, more difficult questions, such as why do we want the world to benefit from our brand and why are we trying to impact positive social change?

5. *Compassion.* In Latin, compassion is defined as "feeling with." One doesn't recognize or accept others' feelings, but feels them. Compassion is having empathetic concern for the suffering of others.

6. *Celebration of diversity.* Compassion is strongly linked to the principle of diversity. Many organizations have diversity programs that involve, for example, putting a token woman or African American on the board of directors or ensuring the workforce contains specified percentages of various ethnic groups, but celebrating diversity means something different. Celebrating diversity means celebrating our differences because they teach us what matters.

7. *Field independence.* Field independence is a term from psychology that means standing against the crowd and being willing to be unpopular for what one believes in. It's a willingness to do it alone, but

only after carefully considering what others have to say. Almost by definition, any visionary leader must sometimes stand alone.

8. *Humility.* Humility is the other necessary side of field independence, whereby a person realizes he or she is an actor in a larger play and might be wrong. Humility makes a leader great, not small. Humility is a sense of being marked by modesty and meekness.

9. *Tendency to ask fundamental "why" questions.* Asking these questions is subversive, and people are often frightened by questions without easy answers. Why are we doing it this way rather than that way? Why am I in this collaboration and why does it exist? Why aren't we doing something else? Answers are a finite game played within boundaries, rules, and expectations. Questions are an infinite game that play with the boundaries and define them.

10. *Ability to reframe.* Reframing refers to the ability to stand back from a situation and look for the bigger picture. One of the greatest problems in the world today is short-term thinking. While connecting with purpose, many people become consumed with

short-term thinking. By focusing on what others want our lives to be, we often go down a dead-end path rather than cultivating our spiritual gifts and talents, coupled with passion, which leads us to purpose.

11. *Positive use of adversity.* This principle is about owning, recognizing, accepting, and acknowledging mistakes. How many of us get trapped in courses of action because the initial step we took was a mistake and we didn't want to lose face by admitting it? Rather than having the courage to acknowledge our error, we pursue the mistaken course of action and dig ourselves deeper into the mess. I have learned a great deal from this. Great passion and energy can be released by saying, "I made a mistake. What I did was wrong, and I'm now going to embark on a different course." Great leaders and social change advocates have the confidence to admit mistakes.

12. *Sense of vocation.* This principle sums up Spiritual Intelligence. Vocation comes from the Latin *vocare*, which means "to be called." Originally, it referred to a calling to God. Today, it often refers to the professions of medicine, education, and law. For

example, in education, universities will become a vocation that appeals to learners with a larger purpose and a desire to make wealth that benefits not only those who create it but also the community and the world. This is what was appealing to me about Walden University's mission on social change when I was exploring doctoral programs. I was looking for an institution with a mission to provide an opportunity for me to grow as a scholar-practitioner and gain the knowledge, coupled with my experience and passion, to impact positive social change in humankind. The rest is history!

Another approach to exploring Spiritual Intelligence is through Cindy Wigglesworth's Deep Change Approach. Wigglesworth (2011) defines Spiritual Intelligence as "the ability to behave with Compassion and Wisdom while maintaining inner and outer peace (equanimity) regardless of the circumstances." Compassion and Wisdom together form the manifestation of Love. "Behave" is important because it focuses on how well we maintain our center, stay calm, and treat others with compassion and wisdom. The statement "regardless of the circumstances" shows that we can maintain our peaceful center and loving behaviors even under great stress. Based on this definition, Wigglesworth framed the skills that represent Spiritual Intelligence in four quadrants below:

© 2004 by Conscious Pursuits, Inc. Reprinted with permission.

The first two quadrants are inner aspects of Spiritual Intelligence; therefore, they are hard for the outer world to see. You can know them about yourself. Other people can only infer your skills in these quadrants based on your behaviors. What others see most about you appears in Quadrants 3 and 4. Quadrants 1 and 2 are interactive and reinforcing. For example, as you discover more about yourself, it is easier to learn about others. As you learn about the beliefs of others, you learn more about yourself. Higher self/ego self-awareness (Quadrant 1) is the predecessor of Quadrant 3 (self/self-mastery). The idea is that until you can hear the voice of your higher self and discern your life purpose and values, it is hard to live by them! Quadrant 4 is dependent upon skill development in the other three quadrants. If you have little self-awareness, you will have little self-mastery. Without self-mastery, it is hard to be wise, compassionate, and peaceful. Similarly, if you cannot understand the beliefs (worldviews) of others, how can you interact with others in a way that is wise or compassionate?

Many systems are driven by four negative motivations: fear, greed, anger, and self-assertion. When these negative emotions control us, we trust both ourselves and others less, and we tend to act from a small place inside ourselves. This inhibits our connection to purpose.

We can change our motivations to be more positive if we are inspired to do so. When practicing Zohar's 12 principles of Spiritual Intelligence, a person may have a greater level of inspiration and motivation to connect to purpose. When we apply the 12 principles of spiritual transformation to our social change collaborations in the field, self-assertion becomes exploration, anger becomes cooperation, craving becomes self-control, fear becomes mastery, and so forth. Our motivations have been raised, and this changes our behavior. As our behavior changes, so do our results and the purpose and meaning of our social change collaborations. We transition from ordinary to extraordinary! In the upcoming chapters, you will meet ordinary people doing extraordinary things to effect change in the world. They come from different frames of reference and have different stories. The key to their stories that started the transformation engine is purpose, hope, and determination. These three characteristics affected their transition from ordinary to extraordinary.

References

Sisk, D., & Torrance, E. (2001). *Spiritual intelligence: Delivering higher consciousness.* Buffalo, NY: Creative Education Foundation Press.

Wolman, R. N. (2003). *Thinking with your soul: Spiritual intelligence and why it matters.* New York, NY: Harmony.

Zohar, D. (2005). Spiritually intelligent leadership. *Leader to Leader, 38*, 45-51. doi:10.1002/ltl.153

4
Chris Daniel, PMP

The Consultant in Jeans
CEO & Founder of Regroup Consulting

It took me 35 years to begin to understand purpose. But I knew what rebounds were!

What is a rebound?

> In sports, a rebound occurs when a player misses a shot/pass and the ball bounces to someone.
>
> In business, a rebound is a shortcoming that leads a person to learn a lesson, go back, and try a more improved approach.
>
> In life, a rebound refers to the uphill process of returning to the original or a better position after a major setback occurs.
>
> In leadership, a rebound occurs when you've shortchanged yourself or your team with your efforts and results, and you have to come back stronger and better while they're giving you the side-eye.

Mental commonalities between the points I just made:

- temporarily detrimental—NEGATIVE
- seemingly impossible to overcome—NEGATIVE
- leaves you with a clean slate—MIDDLE-GROUND
- learn, pivot, come out better—EXTREMELY POSITIVE

■ You think it's detrimental
■ You think it's impossible to overcome
■ You realize you're left with a clean slate
■ You get to learn, pivot, & grow better

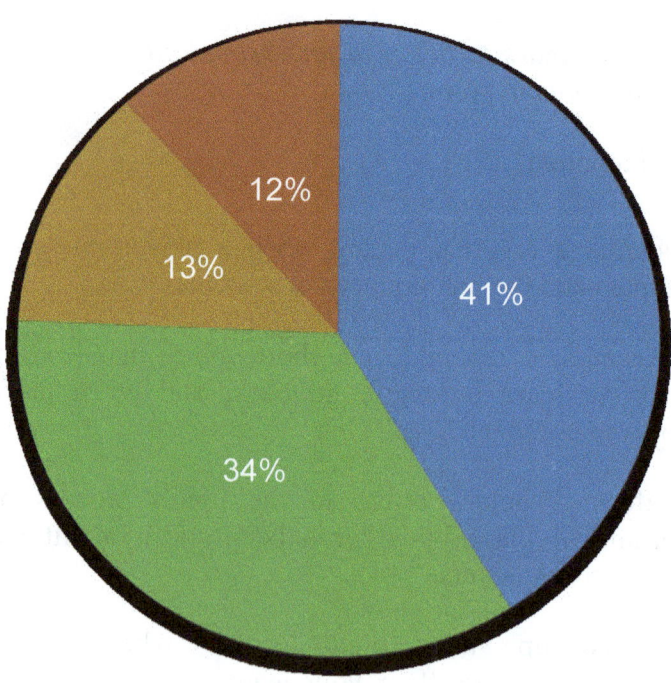

So How Do You Use Rebounds to Your Benefit?

In high school, I won the trophy for best rebounder of my championship basketball team my senior year. That was two decades ago. But a few lessons from my coach have stuck with me all these years:

1. Create a solid foundation when you box out
2. Work smart and hard
3. Commit to always getting better, even when the results don't always show up immediately

Fast forward to today. As an entrepreneur, those lessons have come in handy more than I expected they would.

I remember the lean stages of my business, when it had no money—none. I don't mean I had a low balance in the bank, I mean there was a negative balance. I remember times I asked my ex-wife to use the credit card to get gas for a potential client meeting, and I still didn't get the project!

■ Insert Rebound Stage 1: Go Back and Create a Better, More Solid Foundation

I was pulled in too many directions. I hadn't made up my mind on exactly what I was an expert in, because I knew how to be good at a lot of things. But I wasn't great at any one thing. I had to pull out a sheet of paper and agree with that voice in my head that I was going to master something and sell the hell out of it.

I bounced back. I sharpened my toolbox more and went back. I landed a few corporate training projects and speaking engagements. I think I made about $30,000 my first year in business. I'd paid $32,000 to get started with certifications, travel, and professional designations. So, my first year was a loss, but I kept at it.

Keep at it. This is the true grit stage. And you have to exhibit it or go back and work for someone else.

Then I landed a health care client in Annapolis, Maryland. They asked me to facilitate a series of training sessions for their managers and supervisors. The executive director loved the result! He mentioned he only wanted to work with me for the management-training portion of this particular contract.

Now, if you're in the professional development industry, you know this feeling. You've heard this, right? Long story short: IT DIDN'T HAPPEN. I think I did one or two more projects for them, totaling about $2,500. While that sounds nice, and did help, I didn't hear anything else from them after numerous e-mails, calls, letters, articles, etc.

■ Insert Rebound Stage 2: Work SMARTER (Smarter & Harder)

I knew there was a better way. While I was doing work at that health care organization (and still working on the book, blog, and podcast), I met a VP from a small consulting firm. The firm took an interest in my work and offered me a small project in Baltimore. They'd won a contract and needed minority representation to fulfill it.

Lucky for me, right? Not really. That $10,000 project was awesome—EXCEPT THEY DIDN'T PAY ON TIME. I was paid about 40 days after the work was completed. Talk about lean times! I'd gotten behind on bills, and it was December. My second son had just been born. My ex-wife was home, and I had to go back to work. I was waiting on a payment, and I'd made such an impact that the host firm had offered me a job as a consultant.

Would you have taken it? Consider my mental and financial state:

- marriage on the fringe
- bank account anemic

- holiday season

Damn right I took it. I didn't want to, but I had to. There was a lot of travel involved. Everyone told me to take it, so I did.

■ Insert Rebound Stage 3: Endure and Keep Getting Better. The Results Don't Always Show Up Immediately

When I went back to the drawing board, I decided I would master corporate training. And I committed to learn from other master trainers. I used new techniques in my new role as a consultant and corporate trainer. I operated my business at night, during lunch breaks, and on weekends. I took days off and did small 1-day projects at $800-$1500 a project. I used that money to survive because the salary just paid the bills. I undersold myself, my expertise, and my skill set.

After 6 months with the firm, my ex-wife and I separated. She wanted me to leave, so I did. It wasn't easy, but I did.

I lived in a hotel for about 2 months on rewards points I had earned from the incessant travel. Then, I moved to Extended Stay (i.e., corporate housing) for about 3 months.

I lived with my "aunt" for about a month after that, who graciously allowed me to use her basement. She wasn't really a family member. But she was from my neck of the woods and showed empathy when I needed it most. Then, I lived with a friend who showed me what real friendship is. I tried not to cross the line, but I won't lie and say I didn't. However, I learned a lot about how to be a friend without benefits.

And then my truck broke down! My axle and transmission died . . . in the middle of winter. At this point, my life situations had officially turned into resilience training with a side of P90X on steroids with Sean T. as a Navy Seal!

I was on the way from said friend's house to the airport. I called my insurance and had the truck towed, and she came and took me to the airport. Once at the airport rail station, I hopped on the train and headed for New York, waiting to hear the damage to my vehicle. I got the call the next day: irrecoverable. Well, it was recoverable . . . for $7200. I called my insurance to discuss.

They sent out an adjuster, and called me back the next day: inconclusive. Meanwhile, I was granted a rental. "We're going to send one of our senior adjusters out next week."

That worked for me, since I had the rental, right? I told the adjuster I would be out of town the next week to Miami for work. I wouldn't return until Friday evening, so the rental would have to last the full week. He said, "No problem. We'll call you."

Oh, they called. And said it was inconclusive again! I promise you this is not for dramatic effect. We went around the horn for about 9 weeks, partly due to my travel schedule. The other part due to the shade-tree mechanic who told me he was authorized with my insurance to repair the damages.

During all this, my premise of hope shifted. I'd received an escrow letter from a property I'd purchased in 2007 that had gone to foreclosure.

You know how you get those letters, and you think, "Yeah, right, a mortgage company is going to send me a check for $9,979—when pigs fly." Only, it wasn't a fake! They sent me a check, and it came about a week before I had to turn in the rental.

Long story short, my auto insurance didn't cover the damages because they said it wasn't a "collision." I had a rental car for 67 days! You do the math. A $2200 rental car bill out of my pocket.

After I returned the rental car, I found a used car at the auto auction that fit my speed, and that I could pay for cash. It was 13 years old, but I'd always liked the model. It needed a little work, but it worked. A friend chauffeured me there on a rainy Monday morning. I purchased the vehicle and then headed into the office.

What a winter! But I made it. I rebounded. At the end of 2013, I was finally able to afford my own apartment. Well, kinda sorta, but not really. I was led to an apartment building that I found online and used the remainder of the money to put down the first month's rent and deposit.

God made a way. It wasn't pretty. It wasn't systematic, at least to me. But it happened. I rebounded. I had a car, and a roof, and I was good. I moved into my new place the week of Thanksgiving 2013 and was more grateful than anyone I knew. I even had about $40 in my pocket until I got paid again. I cooked a few things for Thanksgiving and rejoiced.

A few months later, we finalized the divorce. Mixed feelings upon walking in the courtroom to see my ex-wife, three of her girlfriends, and attorney. I represented myself, mainly because I couldn't afford an attorney. I could barely afford to eat.

I remember really blocking the entire court session out and wanting to just ask the judge, "How much?" And it was as if she said, "90% of your earnings!"

After the divorce, things got interesting. It wasn't messy, and I didn't make a stink about the truckload of child support payments I now had to make. For all the days I complained about having to work this job, and build my business on the side, and now make insane payments to my ex-wife, I had a peace of mind that I had not felt in a long time. And as much as I wrestled with the moral implications of divorce, I felt a new sense of freedom.

It took me about 6 months to generate the new Me. I finally accepted me: the better me. I had great days, followed by terrible days. I had some incredible experiences with my son. I lived without cable for about 6 months because I couldn't afford it. I was only home half the month. That time served as the foundation-building process for who I am today.

I finished some personal projects I had begun but had not completed. I finished two eBooks, started an online program, and indulged in social entrepreneurship. I took time to do the sticky, ugly, personal work. The work that most people don't want to do, with tears, and hurt, and questions to God, and side-eyes to the people who disowned me through the process.

The struggle between wanting to tell someone but telling no one for fear of judgment.

THE STRUGGLE IS REAL

That was a defining 6 months for me. I realized I was still a good person, but I needed to be pruned and squeezed and naked to get to the best juice I had to give.

Fast forward to 2016. I'm a full-time entrepreneur with the elasticity of the best rubber bands ever produced. I've become Dr. Chris Daniel by default. And now I realize there was no other way for it to happen.

In August 2015, my first book, *Consult in Jeans*, was released under Tate Publishing. I had poured every ounce of energy, anger, disappointment, and business lessons learned into that book. I finished it while I was in the Extended Stay a year earlier. I'd received the publishing contract while I was homeless.

Rebounding is equivalent to resilience. Both begin with the letter "r." Both are long. Both dictate the tremendous journey you must make to become extraordinary at your life task. I challenge you to engage in your task. The resiliency pays off more than you can ever expect.

Today, I've realized three things:

1. I had to travel through this journey to learn the lessons to become a vehicle of hope for those sitting quiet, in the corner, observing, but not saying a word.
2. The focus had to shift from problems to opportunities through my personal walk in hope and determination. Once that happened, I became a better person.
3. The reaction time to critical events in my life had to go from bitter to better. I had to assess the opportunity to improve my character and then improved results and enlarged territory were mandatory.

Now, I coach top leaders in entrepreneurship and life. I don't claim to be an expert, but I've learned how to learn when I don't know. I've learned to rebound and be bold enough to surround myself with powerful leaders. Most of all, I've learned how much purpose, hope, and determination are part of the makeup of unstoppable leaders. If you want to learn to be unstoppable, use your pain to profit—if not in your life, then in the life of someone else. As I travel across the globe, training and delivering my message, I ask a few questions that are guaranteed to make you even more extraordinary than you already are:

Questions for Resilience Training

1. What's the hardest question you can ask yourself about your journey in life?
2. What nugget can you pull from that story to use as a launchpad to the next level?
3. What one sentence can you craft to help the person quietly sitting in the corner?
4. When will you share it?

5
Thomas Allan Gorry, Brigadier General, USMC

Commandant, Dwight D. Eisenhower School for National Security and Resource Strategy

From student-athlete to warrior-scholar to scholar-practitioner

Life teaches many valuable lessons to those perceptive enough to learn from their experiences and courageous enough to embody them.

I have served in the United States Marine Corps for the past 30 years. This article is not about the Marine Corps per se, but rather the character traits that are the embodiment of the Marine Corps: traits that I cherish, traits that I try my best to live by, and traits that were installed in me through my life experiences—my collegiate wrestling experience in particular. I consider my wrestling experience a defining facet of my life.

By most traditional measures, I was not a very successful wrestler at the University of North Carolina at Chapel Hill (UNC): I was not an Atlantic Coast Conference (ACC) Champion or an All-American. I won about half of my varsity heavyweight wrestling matches, placed in a few collegiate tournaments, and earned valuable team points in the ACC tournament that helped my team win the conference championship my senior season. But the lessons I gained from my wrestling experience far exceeded any of these tangible signs of success—wrestling taught me about myself and life.

Though my wrestling career was brief—2 years at The Hill School and 4 years at UNC—lessons that I learned from this sport have impacted (and will continue to last) a lifetime. My wrestling career was filled with disappointments, unfulfilled goals, and painful memories; at the time, it was filled with an immense pride, a sincere respect, and a deep determination. It was through dealing with these negative and positive components that the true value in my collegiate wrestling experience rests. The intangible qualities of discipline, dedication, devotion, resilience, and commitment that emerged during these formative years became the foundation of my life, as I grew to appreciate their value in character development.

I fell in love with the sport immediately upon my first encounter on the wrestling mat. I was coerced into joining my high school wrestling team by the captain of our football team, but I was hooked by the fierce competition and extreme demands associated with this individual and team sport. I was determined to master this highly competitive sport and completely dedicated myself to its physical and mental challenges. I took each loss personally, as a sign of letting myself and my teammates down. Preparation for each match became as important as the match itself. I enthusiastically strove to improve my performance, which enhanced my understanding of my competitive nature. I became aware of my strengths and weaknesses, and adopted a wrestling style in which I tried to maximize the former and compensate for the later. I promised myself I would always be in better shape than my opponent and that I would never quit, regardless of the circumstances. I defined winning not only on the outcome of each contest but also in terms of my effort and attitude.

My membership on and contribution to the UNC wrestling team was another aspect in my personal experience and development. Winning wrestling matches was not the only way to contribute to the team; I demonstrated leadership through my dedication, perseverance, and determination in confronting the challenges of competing on the collegiate level. As a non-scholarship athlete, I thoroughly appreciated and sought to make the most out of the wrestling experience. I was fully committed to the team and my teammates. In response, I received a sense of belonging and enduring friendships forged through shared hardships.

After graduating from UNC with a bachelor of science in business administration, I moved home to help my family work through a crisis; my father had recently lost his job, and I had two sisters and a brother in college. The timing was not right for me to begin a professional career; instead, I worked for a merchandise distributor loading trucks at night. I did not get depressed or lose hope; rather, I gave myself 6 months to find my path in life. As I worked each night landing trucks, I thought and prayed about my personal goals, objectives, and dreams. I determined that my life's path would have purpose and meaning.

I decided to pursue a professional career in an organization founded on the same personal qualities and character traits that I had learned as a collegiate student athlete—the United States Marines Corps. From the moment I began military service in this legendary organization, I was expected to adhere to its core values of Honor, Courage, and Commitment and live by its motto: Semper Fidelis (Always Faithful). I purposefully chose a career that would challenge me both mentally and physically, and I pursued military service with the same dogged determination that I had applied in my wrestling career. I strove to be the best military officer that I could be and to be always mindful of my reputation, position, and character. I confronted challenges head-on and I never compromised my personal integrity, moral standards, or code of conduct. My reward has been advancement to assignments of increasing responsibility and acceptance in an organization imbued with a warrior spirit and chivalrous culture.

My personal life mirrors my professional career with regard to my devotion, commitment, and dedication. I cherish my family and am blessed to have a loving and supportive spouse and four tremendous children. Despite the demands of a professional military career, I have remained true to my wedding vows and committed to my paternal responsibilities. I met my wife during the 6 months I worked on the loading docks, and upon receiving my commission in the Marine Corps, we got engaged. I bought the engagement ring with the money that I had earned at Officer Candidate School (OCS) in Quantico, Virginia. Throughout my training, she served as a source of hope and inspiration, and throughout my career, she has been my companion, confidant, and best friend.

The lessons in fortitude, courage, and mental toughness instilled in me during my college wrestling career enabled me to succeed in this demanding and challenging course. I regarded OCS as a right-of-passage for my destiny, and I was determined to pass this important crucible. In fact, these character values have defined my approach and purpose to life. They have provided an ethical framework for my personal conduct and instilled a sense of honor, integrity, and fidelity in me that underscores my existence. I treasure my wrestling experience; it enabled me to develop the character, resilience, and purpose to overcome the varied demands of life. It also enabled me to achieve a level of success personally and professionally. I was promoted to the rank of Brigadier General in August 2012 and inducted into the National Wrestling Hall of Fame in May 2013. Learning these character traits is only half the story; I was able to apply the valuable lessons that I learned as a collegiate student-athlete to become a warrior-scholar and pursue my doctorate degree as a scholar-practitioner.

Throughout my military career, I committed myself to advancing my education through both formal academic schools as well as an ardent professional reading program. I considered learning to be an essential part of my preparation for the increased demands and responsibilities associated with my professional development. My academic pursuits enhanced my knowledge of global economics, political affairs, and international relations, which enabled me to have a better understanding of the increasing complexities of our national security and more ably serve in assignments in Europe, Asia, and the Middle East. In addition, my dedicated study of military history allowed me to learn valuable lessons from previous commanders and conflicts, which enabled me to better lead in austere, hostile, and dangerous settings. In essence, my commitment to education made me a more capable, confident, and competent military officer.

My educational pursuits have included both military and civilian programs, as each complemented my professional and personal objectives. As a young adult, I was fortunate to attend a prestigious private high school (The Hill School), which instilled in me an appreciation and strong desire for higher academic studies. My passion to learn has enabled me to obtain several graduate degrees and teach in both military and civilian environments and continues to drive me to pursue a doctoral degree—the pinnacle of advanced education.

The graduate degrees I earned from Central Michigan University (MSA) and Webster University (MBA) enhanced my knowledge and understanding of organizational management, which enabled me to serve in senior staff assignments and teach undergraduate business courses. Attaining a graduate degree in national security strategy from the National Defense University strengthened my understanding of national strategy, which enabled me to assume high-level assignments in Europe and Afghanistan and serve as an adjunct faculty member for the Marine Corps University.

Besides preparing me for important military postings, my academic credentials have allowed me to obtain leadership positions at both the Marine Corps University and the National Defense University. My current assignment as the Commandant of the Dwight D. Eisenhower School for National Security and Resource Strategy capitalizes on my military experience as a logistician and my academic studies in business and national strategy. This assignment enables me to pursue a doctorate degree in management on a research topic that explores these areas of interest.

I consider myself a life-long learner and regard an advanced degree as essential to not only reaching the highest positions in my profession but also establishing a strong foundation for my eventual transition from the active military to a senior executive or corporate consultant. My educational achievements have worked in conjunction with my career objectives; therefore, I decided to pursue a doctor of philosophy in management program with Walden University. I specifically joined an academic program designed to provide career professionals the opportunity to exchange ideas, share experiences, and explore new concepts through concentrated research as a scholar-practitioner. The linkage between the two disciplines of academic and career reinforces the learning process and leads to a more thorough understanding of the concepts through realistic, practical application.

I chose the military as my professional career and served on active duty for most of my adult life to make a difference in the world. I am pursuing a doctorate degree to further my contribution to society by using my passion for education to explore new domains in leadership and management and their effect on national security.

6
Kenneth Taylor, PhD

Founder and Principle for Partnership for Educational Growth Systems (PEGS)

Overcoming Rejection with Resilience: Flexible yet Firm

We must be willing to get rid of the life we've planned, so as to have the life that is waiting for us.
—Joseph Campbell

Purpose is something that not even the wisest person can confidently determine. I view purpose as a supernatural, superhuman, spiritually driven determination that is far beyond our control. I also see it as a gift that is given if and when we decide to adhere to the message that is articulated. We are given signs from very early on in our lives about what our purpose is. From the types of materials we enjoy reading, places we like to visit, and people we surround ourselves with. If we are lucky, we discover our purpose early on. If it takes time, then our purpose is often manifested in the things that we are passionate about. Our passions are those compelling emotions and cravings that light a fire inside of us. I believe those emotions and cravings are merely hints guiding us to our purpose.

I have learned that I am extremely passionate about helping others, more specifically as it relates to educational attainment. To delve deeper, I would say my passion lies within providing educational opportunities and resources for marginalized individuals to reach their goals. Thus, in my various activities through my work, volunteering, mentoring, and casual conversation, I walk in the passions and cravings that surround education. I am not quite sure if my full purpose has been revealed or if I have heard exactly what my story will be. However, as I move closer to my purpose, I have observed that everything I do is influenced and forever changed by the contributions of my passion and sincerity.

I was born on January 28, 1980, to a 16-year-old mother and a 15-year-old father. I am the oldest of four children: three boys and one girl. I am the eldest grandchild on both sides of my families, as well as the oldest great grandchild. Never did I imagine the task that was ahead of me in leading the younger generations of children coming through my family, though my journey was made easy, as my family offered all the love support and guidance needed to achieve my goals. At the age of 3, my parents enrolled me in private school. It was not without a financial burden, but my parents were determined to provide me the best education possible. I remember learning my alphabet and often recited them very loudly to my parents. At that time, I developed a foundation of confidence and pleasure in academic achievement.

The countdown to obtain my doctorate began in 1985, when I was 5. I recall my parents asking, "What do you want be when you grow up," and I boldly replied, "I want to be a doctor." I cannot quite remember what inspired me or sparked the idea to become a doctor, but I believe it came from an innate desire to help people. This idea later manifested into me wanting to deliver babies, because I thought that's what doctors do. That's when they gave me the nickname "Dr. J." My parents and family carefully nurtured my desire by flooding my mind with books and giving me the opportunity to participate in various extracurricular activities.

I was never pressured to make A's and B's, nor would my parents have punished me for making anything less, but there was something in me that loved achieving. Achievement was easy for me; it was the thing to do. Throughout grade school, I made the honor roll and received numerous certificates, awards, and trophies, in addition to participating in extracurricular activities and clubs.

In the 20 years after my declaration, a number of life-changing and life-determining events happened that made me the man I am today, and I attribute my success and resilience directly to those incidents. In 1987, my family suffered a great loss, as our house burned to the ground, and we were left with nothing more than a few family portraits from my parents' wedding. Seeing everything my family worked so hard for buried under black ash changed my perspective. Money, clothes, jewelry, and furniture were all gone, but the most significant symbol of family was spared: the union of my parents.

Lesson: Nothing is forever. Cherish what's important and learn to understand and let go of the rest.

> *Abraham Lincoln once said, "In the end it's not the years in your life that count, it's the life in your years."*

In 1991, as a new student to my middle school, I boldly ran for vice president of my sixth-grade class with the encouragement of my homeroom and history teacher. After my speech and the dead silence in the crowd, I remember walking across the stage back to my seat and feeling like I wanted to run home. I pretty much knew I was not going to win, and I did not.

By the spring of 1997, my junior year of high school, I had worked very diligently for 3 years to be one of the best trombonists in the band. I practiced my music and my steps religiously, and I maintained good relationships with the band staff and other band members. I had served as the section leader for the prior year. I was certain I would be one of the few chosen to serve as drum major for the Marching Panther Band, but I was not. Crushed and confused, I was able to recall at least one incident that led to the decision. My initial response was to quit the band, and I did. One summer and life-changing car accident later, I boldly rejoined the band, and that spring I received a band scholarship to Tennessee State University (TSU).

> *I never really viewed obstacles as things that blocked my way; I always just believed they were mysterious doors to my destiny.*

Webster's (2015) defines hope as a desire with the accompanied expectation of fulfilment that something good will happen. Based on that definition, I am very cautious about operating in hope. Hope comes with too many uncontrollable variables, and a person cannot rely on with the expectation that something good will happen. My faith is the most significant a determinant for my journey through life. One of Webster's (2015) definitions of faith is "complete trust." Complete trust in someone or something, or even God. It's an allegiance to the intent of things to come. Some believers have coined the phrase "What is for me, is for me." Many people walk through life with the idea that as long as they have faith, everything will work out.

By the time I enrolled at TSU, I had decided to major in physical therapy, as becoming an obstetrician would not work well with my fear of blood. By the first semester of my sophomore year, I was heartbroken to learn that several of the reasons I chose TSU were stripped away or nonexistent. The fraternities that I wanted to join were not on the yard, and the program I selected was disbanded to develop the accreditation standards of similar programs. I always kept my faith that I would succeed at completing my college education. My determination to graduate within 4 years did not change in spite of those obstacles, and on May 11, 2002, I was graduated with honors with a degree in psychology.

As I have pursued each of my goals, I did so by walking in faith and by knowing and trusting that with hard work, things will work out as they should. This means that my path is not always so easily plotted by the actions and activities that I participate in, but that there is a divine order to the way and when things happen. Having that trust gives me hope for my future endeavors and thus pushes me to move forward. For me, hope is simply putting faith to action. I am most hopeful that my passion for helping to develop future generations is rewarded with thousands of individuals who are able to walk in their purpose and achieve their goals.

I was asked by a close friend if faith could be influenced, and my answer was "Yes it can, with hope and action." Many of us pray for things to happen. We even say that we have faith that things will happen. I believe that no good deed or great feat is achieved without work on the part of the dreamer. In the Bible, there is a scripture that says, "Now faith is the substance of things hoped for, the evidence of things not seen." (Hebrews 11:1). This scripture does not tell me not to work hard and do my due diligence to achieve my goals. It means I should not worry, but stay the course.

Faith is a belief; it is spiritual. Hope is a verb that is manifested in works.

To understand what it means to be extraordinary is a journey that I learned starts at the end of my boundaries. The key principle is to always stretch beyond what is comfortable. At various times in my life, I experienced a sense of complacency. I blamed the failings on my surroundings, not realizing that I needed to change, not my surroundings. I also realized that my inability to get out of those moments was completely related to my fear of failure and ultimately my fear of change. At those times, I had to remind myself that the only constant in this life is change. If I am to grow in the way that has been determined for me, I would have to change or get left behind. This expansion of thought did not come without a cost. For everything that is gained, there is a loss. The loss could be removing people from our lives that no longer serve a purpose, removing activities, or removing doubt. Gains come with a cost.

When asked how my territory has been enlarged as a result of my doctoral degree, I laugh. As I stated before, the journey from ordinary to extraordinary is one that begins at the end of our boundaries. I began my doctoral journey in the fall of 2005, at the age of 25. As stated, I have always been an academician at heart. I would not say that I was naturally smart, but I worked very diligently to always make the grade and be successful. I had no clue that the doctoral process would be the opposite of anything I had ever experienced. The transition from my master's degree program was a piece of cake. The course work was a walk in the park. But there is something about the doctoral process that transforms you. It is one of the most humbling experiences in the world.

Once you get beyond your course work, you realize that the clock is all yours. You no longer have a calendar, due dates, or tests to take. The test becomes your willingness and steadfastness to (a) stay the course and (b) finish. I have always been one that works well under pressure, and I appreciate a deadline to keep me on track. There was no pressure, deadlines, or tracks during this process. It was all me, and no one cared that I completed the process more than I did.

For the first time, I was on my own. I had reached a major boundary: lack of structure. I struggled with the process for about two semesters, which is almost a year. I could not seem to focus and structure a path that aligned with my goals and the task at hand. I reached out to friends and my advisor, but no one could help me.

One day I woke up frustrated and even irritated that I was not progressing the way I thought I should. I had a long conversation with myself during which I finally determined that someone did this before me and someone will do this after me. That understanding was all the motivation I needed. It reminded me that God will never put more on me that than what I can achieve. I knew that I had come too far and worked too hard. It was not a matter of if I would do it, but when. I had faith that I would complete the task, and I had to put a plan of action in place to make it a reality.

I carry that understanding and mind-set everywhere I go. I instill it in my colleagues, my peers, and my family. There is nothing new about what we are doing; someone has already proven that it can be done. The goal is to do it, do it well, and have fun doing it. I take on every challenge with this mind-set, and my positive spirit gives everyone around me the boost needed to achieve the goal.

I often have conversations with people about their goals and the obstacles that they have encountered. It is always so amazing to hear people talk about what they want to achieve but who are so afraid to go beyond their boundaries and make the leap of faith to be where they want to be. It's always an interesting conversation because people talk as if they are so conflicted with where they are, but they offer so many reasons why going where they want to be is too difficult. I explain that the conflict you feel is your left self telling your right self to do it. That conflicting feeling never goes away. It can get stronger and louder, or it can be silenced by excuses. For the lucky, that sound gets so loud that you have no choice but to stretch beyond your comfort zone. That moment makes high-ranking executives walk away from 18 years with a company. At that moment, the introverted intellect walks before a crowd of 10,000 people and speaks with the confidence of a rock star. That is the moment we all wait for but dread because we are afraid that it might not turn out the way we planned.

I have learned that regardless of how it turns out, not trying feels worse. I can attribute my wins to my ability to take a loss. I contribute my success to all the failures I have encountered. I contribute my prosperity to the adverse situations I encountered again and again. Ironically, the journey would not have been more rewarding if it were not for the noes that made the yeses so much more meaningful.

References

Faith. (2015). Retrieved from http://www.merriam-webster.com/dictionary/faith

Hope. (2015). Retrieved from http://www.merriam-webster.com/dictionary/hope

7
Deborah George-Feres, PhD, PCC

Founder & Executive Coach
Indigo Coaching Systems

Difficulties are not deterrents—they can ignite determination

A quote from one of my favorite authors, M. Scott Peck, summarizes the intricate difficulties of the human existence. This statement explains the complexities of the human experience in a profound way:

> Life is difficult. This is a great truth, one of the greatest truths. It is a great truth because once we truly see this truth, we transcend it. Once we truly know that life is difficult—once we truly understand and accept it—then life is no longer difficult. Because once it is accepted, the fact that life is difficult no longer matters.

This quote resonated with me because the pursuit of a doctoral degree is a difficult endeavor in itself, but when compounded with life's challenges, it increases the degree of difficulty. In pursuit of the degree, I initially anticipated a difficult journey—one that would stretch me beyond my current intellectual capabilities and outside my comfort zone. Cognizant of this knowledge, I expected some difficulties. However, I did not foresee the number of challenges that were to come. During those 4 years, I experienced a significant personal challenge in the death of my beloved mother. Her death was crippling, because at times, I felt I could not continue the journey. Nonetheless, during my despair, an important event occurred that reminded me of my mother's strength. In that moment, I felt her strength envelop me and I used it to stay on the course to completion. I was able to complete my doctorate not only due to the strength I drew from my mother's spirit but also because of my determination and passion.

The concept of passion appears elusive at times, especially when it is compared to a feeling. For me, passion is not simply a feeling. Instead, I perceive passion as innate, intimate, and intuitive. Passion is innate because it resides within oneself. Whether it is explicit or soon to be discovered, it exists within an individual's soul. The soul elevates it to a person's consciousness. This consciousness cultivates passion through experiences and environment.

Another term I link to passion is intimate. This is because sometimes passion is only experienced by the individual, although it can be made visible to others. For example, a musician may be able to create a beautiful composition of lyrics and melodies that others whose passion is not music or who are not musicians can appreciate. Similarly, the works of art produced by an artist may elicit passion in others, which means that artists can transfer passion through their work.

If you ask artists to describe the passion they feel when crafting artifacts, it may be difficult for them to articulate. They may not be able to explain how they were able to transfer their passion into a creative expression. In this context, I believe that passion is an intimate concept that artists make explicit. In contrast, when I perceive passion as an intuitive concept, it is known only to oneself and remains hidden to others. As such, my definition of passion is a ubiquitous concept that comprises the essence of an individual's soul elevated through consciousness and self-awareness. That consciousness facilitates action, which allows the individual to navigate through life's journey with passion, despite difficulties. In a nutshell, passion leads to purpose and purpose produces determination.

Thus, a relationship exists between purpose and determination. Without purpose, there is no determination. Within the hierarchy of the three concepts, passion, purpose, and determination, determination is the driver and purpose is the passenger. Together, they morph into a unified state that allows a person to experience euphoria, happiness, and self-fulfillment, irrespective of life's difficulties. When purpose and determination are combined, there is a sense of hope that follows. Hope is useful when visualizing possibilities. Without hope, executing life goals and traversing through life would be difficult. Thus, hope is a fundamental element of determination, particularly self-determination.

According to Deci and Ryan's (1985) self-determination theory, people are driven by intrinsic or extrinsic factors that support or diminish motivation. Deci and Ryan defined motivation as a composite of determination and attainment of psychological needs such as autonomy, competence, and relatedness. Without determination, a person's willpower would most likely recede, thereby making it difficult to navigate through life's perils. The theorists posited that there is an interplay between motivation and determination. Motivation is the force that propels determination. It is the impetus to action and the development and maintenance of determination. As a doctoral student, I was determined to complete my degree. This was my intrinsic motivation because it was an internal drive. I was not forced or coerced by any external forces. My intrinsic motivation was transformed into self-determination, which facilitated my ability to function effectively under challenging conditions.

Several years ago, I gave a talk to a group of business leaders and entrepreneurs on moving from functional to exceptional. I asked the audience to define the difference between functional and exceptional. The feedback was fascinating because the audience defined functional as fulfillment of purpose or function and defined exceptional as outstanding or above average. I then asked the audience, by show of hands, how many of them would define themselves as exceptional. To my surprise, only a few people raised their hands. I surmised that the ones who did not raise their hands only saw themselves as average, or normal, human beings. This placed the importance of my talk at a higher level than I initially anticipated. I could not fathom why a group of whom I perceived to be successful business people perceived themselves as average. However, not too long after, the reasons were made clear to me. I learned that many entrepreneurs and business leaders, particularly those operating small or start-up businesses, are juggling many different roles. They are usually overwhelmed by the multitude of tasks associated with these different roles. Thus, they carry with them the constant feeling of incompletion, meaning that they focused on unfinished tasks, rather than celebrating their successes.

As such, they could not see themselves as exceptional individuals, which led to negative self-perceptions and created a mind-set of ineffectiveness. They did not have a positive perception of how their products or services benefited their customers. Thus, it was evident that in order for these entrepreneurs and business leaders to move from functional to exceptional, they had to change their mind-set. They needed to eliminate negative self-talk and open up their consciousness to a new way of thinking. They needed to change their conventional definitions of success. From an interactive exercise, many of these business leaders began to change their self-perceptions of mediocrity, and they were able to define success as the quality of their products or services, to value their customers' loyalty, and to accept the natural process of growth and development.

In that talk, I offered several principles to move from functional to exceptional. The principles are as follows:

1. Make the right choices. In his book, *Your Life: Why It Is the Way It Is, And What You Can Do About It*, Bruce McArthur stated that your experiences are derived from your choices, and those choices create your life. Making the right choices may not get you where you need to be fast, but you will get there with a clear conscience.
2. Set your goals and aspirations in accordance with your spirit. Spirit is the essence of self. Knowing who you are allows you to stand your ground, even if you are the odd man out.
3. Face your fears. Avoiding your fears will only delay the inevitable and bring more discomfort later.
4. Increase self-awareness. As humans, we are constantly changing and evolving. You are not the same person you were a year or 10 years ago. Thus, it is important to do a periodic self-check to relearn your evolving self.
5. Utilize your intuition. In a society where numbers are regarded as facts, intuition is perceived as a less credible source. However, intuition is a source of knowledge and a guide into the unknown or unfamiliar. Trust that gut feeling or body sensation more often.

6. Develop a success-based strategy. Your success-based strategy is a long-term plan of action for achieving your life's goals. It consists of the following components:
    - Helpfulness: Make yourself as useful as possible to others. Find out what people's needs are and help meet those needs, either as a business owner or as a volunteer.
    - Mission: Develop a personal and professional mission statement. Your mission statement is important because it directs your path.
    - Action: Be action-oriented. Don't wait to be told what to do or for things to happen. Make things happen! Get things done! In David Allen's book, *Getting things done: The art of stress-free productivity*, he described an easy method to store, track, retrieve, process, review, and organize all types of information. This book was an eye-opener for me and helped me organize my life as a business owner and a doctoral student.

These principles are valuable and can help you transform from functional to exceptional, become indispensable, and become successful. In addition, apply daily affirmations. Affirmations are great motivators and can quiet negative self-talk. They are also healing vehicles by which you can free yourself from overdependence on others' opinions of you. Using daily affirmations can help you face your fears and take charge of the present with a less obstructed view of your reality. Repeating daily affirmations will help reduce others' faulty views of you and your own negative self-image and will allow you to produce a positive self-perception.

Give yourself permission to grow, change, take risks, rise up, or fall, so that you are able to create a better life for you and your loved ones and positively impact the world. As a doctoral student, I have been stretched intellectually. As a business owner, I have taken remarkable risks. From these risks and challenges, I have grown immensely. I gave myself permission to grow and be patient, not just with the doctoral process, but also with my business and myself. Being patient with myself was an important lesson, because I had to relearn how to learn, while not being too hard on myself. I needed to learn how to learn in a doctoral program, within an online, self-directed environment. I needed to add additional skills to my repertoire to be a successful scholarly practitioner.

Another important lesson learned is that preparation and organization are needed to write the dissertation. Preparation is paramount to the development of the dissertation, and organization is critical to execution. Being organized and patient allowed me to learn the difference between excellence and perfection. Excellence is the quality of one's work that sets that individual apart from the average person. Perfection is the act of reaching the highest attainable standard established by the university. At the onset of my doctoral journey, I was working from the mind-set of the latter. However, I soon learned that it was an elusive goal. More important, working to achieve perfection was also a time-eater. Based on that understanding, I strove for excellence, which then created a mental shift and allowed me to achieve a standard of excellence, which is a concept I now apply when training for marathons and providing services to my clients.

Last, as an individual who possessed a deep appreciation for knowledge and a commitment to positive change, it was important for me to receive my doctorate from Walden University. Walden's mission is to advance positive social change. That mission mirrors my own personal values, and as such, Walden was the ideal university to advance my knowledge and promote my commitment. As a Walden' doctoral graduate, I am now equipped with the practical and theoretical knowledge to influence leaders positively by directing the organizational change process, conducting effective coach training programs, and heightening leaders' self-awareness that produces organizational effectives. In closing, my doctoral degree has prepared me for helping leaders become exceptional people.

References

Allen, D. (2001). *Getting things done: The art of stress-free productivity*. New York, NY: Viking.

Deci, E., & Ryan, R. (1985). *Intrinsic motivation and self-determination in human behavior*. New York, NY: Plenum.

McArthur, B. (1993). *Your life: Why it is the way it is, and what you can do about it: Understanding the universal laws*. Virginia Beach, VA: A.R.E. Press.

Peck, M. (1978). *The road less traveled: A new psychology of love, traditional values, and spiritual growth*. New York, NY: Simon and Schuster.

8
Dr. Kimberly Dixon-Lawson

Department of Veteran Affairs

An extraordinary life does not include short cuts. It is a journey full of the high and lows of each experience.

Transitioning from Ordinary to Extraordinary

I believe that every person possesses a purpose for being on Earth. Some people know their purpose rather quickly in life, while others take much longer to realize it. The question can be posed, "Do you choose your purpose or does your purpose choose you?" Perhaps it can be either, perhaps both. Regardless of how you arrive at the answer, one concept remains true: without passion, your purpose is in danger of never being fulfilled. I find that in every aspect of my life, I conduct myself with both purpose and passion. It is my goal to have my life serve as a testament to others who may need direction or guidance on how to arrive at their own truth.

Permission to Find Purpose

I realized at a young age that I enjoy being in the company of others. I am most comfortable in a setting where there is a free flow of ideas and an atmosphere of acceptance where I am both a speaker and a listener. Learning is evolutionary over time, and the way I tend to process information differs as I mature. There is more openness to the process, and I am more available mentally and emotionally to receive new information. I attribute this trait to growing up in a household where I was encouraged to be adventurous, with parents who relished my curiosity. With my own children, I try to mimic the same behavior by giving them permission to be who they are with complete acceptance and unconditional love.

As an African American child growing up in rural Mississippi, I had no grasp of just how scarce educational and employments opportunities were at that time. It wasn't until I began to grow into young adulthood that I realized the obstacles I would have to overcome to fulfill my purpose of becoming a productive member of society. Regardless of what those obstacles were or may have been, one constant that remained was that my upbringing kept me focused on what steps I needed to take to attain a certain level of success. My parents taught me to aim as high as possible and to know that any goals I ever set for myself were never unattainable. My mind-set has never been to let my surroundings dictate my purpose in life. No matter what was going on outside of my household, my parents' love and adoration for me and my two siblings kept us in line and prepared us for whatever life brought our way.

Finding Passion in My Purpose

During my undergraduate program at Jackson State University while I was earning a bachelor's of science in psychology, I became enthralled with the biology of people. Human behavior is fascinating to me, and I found myself wanting to learn more. Whether it is the mundaneness of everyday life or the intricacies of abnormal psychology, I was aware of the likelihood of my choosing a profession that would provide the opportunity to interact with people from all walks of life. During my junior year in college, I had the chance to work as a case manager in a group home for adults with serious mental illness.

From the beginning, I was aware that this type of employment is not for everyone. However, I welcomed the challenge and reveled in the chance to work in a helping profession. I had visions of making a difference and impacting the lives of the consumers who occupied the group home. From a professional standpoint, I wanted to learn as much about the field of psychology as the job would allow.

The residents were adults who'd at one time been inpatients at the state mental hospital and had earned the right to transition into group home care. They presented with a dichotomy of different experiences and diagnoses, each different from the last. I was responsible for documenting daily progress, providing medications, overseeing meals, chores, and maintaining a sense of stability during my 8-hour shift. We got to know each other very well, and it was hard to see them cycle through the home when it was time to leave.

This job set the tone for the rest of my career. I knew that I would continue to help others in some capacity. I had the ability to see each consumer as a human being with real and valuable human experience. It meant so much to me that I had been allowed to be a part of their lives. The surprising revelation for me was that they impacted my life just as much as I did theirs. This job is where I found my passion and helped further develop the purpose set forth for my life's journey.

In regards to career development, I made it a priority to speak and spend time with the licensed counselors and clinical staff. I developed a list of questions that I wanted to get answered in regard to relevant certifications and licenses, potential next steps, and the possibility of mentorship. I was tenacious in my approach and unapologetic in demeanor. This was my chance, and I was determined to build a solid foundation on which to grow. Fortunately, there were several clinicians who took the time to guide my early development, which I now know is an essential building block of giving back. I vowed that when the opportunity presented itself, I would do the same.

Hope and Determination: Quest for Fulfillment

My early years as an undergraduate came and went. Shortly after earning a bachelor's degree, I continued my education by obtaining a master's in rehabilitation counseling. I continued to work in the helping professions as a school-based therapist in a community mental health center and later a vocational counselor with both the State of Texas and the U.S. Department of Veteran Affairs. I've spent the last 10 years of my career serving this nation's veterans as a counselor and now as a health systems specialist. I could not be more proud of this honor. My career has brought many awards and recognitions, and I feel positive that working to give a voice to vulnerable populations is my intended purpose. Despite this fact, I still felt there was more for me to do both personally and professionally. The decision to pursue my doctoral degree was both frightening and exciting; one that would test my level of drive and determination. In addition, as a wife, mother, and full-time career woman, I feared that I lacked the time. Despite these facts, I was dedicated to pursing this lifelong dream. This led to my decision to choose an online doctoral program.

From the start of the journey, I made a promise: No matter what happens, I would never give up. I had always been an excellent student, but found myself very intimidated by the level of work required. Becoming a critical thinker and scholar-practitioner were foreign tasks that would require a new way of looking at the world. For the first time in years, I doubted my ability to rise to the occasion. I was fearful of my worthiness in reaching the next level. However, what I lacked in confidence, I had in both hope and determination. One of the strategies that I adopted was reaching out to fellow doctoral learners in the online classroom and building connections while attending academic residencies.

Taking Advantage of Networking

Being a part of an academic environment is exhilarating. It's alive with energy and excitement. The academic residency is a great example of this environment, especially as a first-year doctoral student. This is where I found my footing and became fully committed to the process. I paired myself with like-minded students. I sought out the professors that made the biggest impact on my learning experience and continued to keep in touch throughout my years in the program. I challenged myself and remained connected to others who challenged me as well. I modeled the behavior of those I considered to be successful, whether as students or faculty members, while envisioning the future I'd planned. It was my personal responsibility to see my dream through to the end, and I was fully prepared to make the sacrifices to become a doctoral degree holder.

The Transition from Ordinary to Extraordinary

When I received the call that I'd passed the oral defense and completed the requirements of my program, it was a surreal moment. I first shared the news with my husband and children, then other family and friends. Since 2009, many changes have occurred in my professional life. The one that made the most impact stems from the vow that I made during my own journey. I am now an adjunct professor in a health services doctoral program. I have the opportunity to help other students reach their goals of transitioning from ordinary to extraordinary. One of my responsibilities is serving as chair and committee member for dissertation students, which is a huge undertaking that brings me great joy. When one of my mentees makes it across the finish line and becomes a new doctor, I feel a sense of accomplishment akin to my own. I have fulfilled my promise to give back and touch the lives of others.

Conclusion

As I reflect over my personal journey from ordinary to extraordinary, there are several key lessons that stand out:

1. Each person is in control of his or her own learning and success. Challenges and obstacles will undoubtedly be a part of the journey, but it is up to each person to persevere.

2. Visualize the future you have in mind and plan accordingly.
3. Each person's journey is different. You must chart your own path.
4. Relish every step of the journey. There's a lesson in it all.

9
Dr. Pettis Perry

Educator

My Journey, My Truth, My Peace

Anyone considering a doctoral program of study must ascertain his or her motivation for doing so ahead of entering the chosen program if that person wants to succeed, because the arduous and taxing journey can take 3 to 5 years or longer to complete. The process culminates with a major research project that demonstrates a high level of competency in a very narrowly defined area that produces a highly specialized body of knowledge for the initiate, resulting in deep expertise in the chosen area of interest. Among other things, each person has to determine for him or herself whether the reason for pursuing a doctorate is to be called doctor or because of a deep and undying passion for the chosen subject matter. This is an important decision because anyone pursuing a doctorate will live with that degree for the rest of his or her life. The outcome of this decision makes a difference in terms of that person's approach to the program of study and to the way that person will carry him or herself after donning the symbolic mantle of the chosen discipline. I was deeply passionate about my subject matter and did not care at all about being called doctor. I simply wanted to increase my knowledge base about something that fascinated me about how the world works in practice and to hone my skill sets to become a more capable practitioner. In the beginning, I was unaware how much the lenses through which I would learn to see the world would dramatically change my life, and therefore my perspective of the fishbowl within which I lived.

My own program of study began with a thought provoking orientation in which the facilitator, who later became my favorite professor, spoke to all of us about the journey that lay before us. He admonished all of us to think deliberately about the demands that a doctoral program places on individual students, their families, friendships, as well as the colleagues with whom they work. Little did I know that during the final class in my program of study that my favorite professor would ask me to comment in front of my classmates about my thoughts that final night. In the process of recounting my thoughts, I found myself finishing my program of study where I had begun during my orientation. I realized that he had been right: Some of my classmates had dropped out of their programs, some had divorced their spouses, many of us lost friendships, and I had difficulties with some of those with whom I worked. In addition, I understood in those final moments of my final class that I was no longer the person I was at the beginning of my journey, and those around me would forever see me differently simply because I would be called doctor after I graduated.

My own journey toward wearing a doctoral hood actually began in 1976 during my undergraduate graduation ceremonies on the football field at San Francisco State University. On that day, the first students to be hooded were three new doctoral graduates who were being conferred their degrees. As I watched their hooding, I was enthralled with their powder-blue-lined regalia that I later learned was the color awarded to those receiving their doctorates of education. The powder blue resonated with my soul for some reason that I could not explain, and some 20 years later, I too received a powder blue hood as part of my graduation from the University of San Francisco.

But, I am getting ahead of myself, so let me go back to my early beginnings. I was born into a family with parents who were activists. My father had only 15 months of formal education, yet he taught himself how to read and write, and by the time he died, we had a 3,000-book library in our home. While my father began his life as a sharecropper, he later became a laborer, labor organizer, speaker, and author. My mother, who had a high school education, was a bookkeeper by trade and an amateur artist, and she wrote several unpublished manuscripts, including one about Robert Smalls who, during the Civil War, stole a Confederate Navy ship and turned it over to the Union Navy. When I was in elementary and junior high school, she periodically asked me to help her with her bookkeeping, which laid the early foundation for my professional career to be able to construct budgets and perform successfully as an executive leader where many of my predecessors and peers failed. My mother also took my father's dictation to type his manuscripts for publication. The fact that my father was self-taught yet highly successful and the efforts my parents made to expose their three sons to an array of experiences with diverse cultures and family friends took away from my life equation any reasons for not being successful that I might be able to conjure up for myself. Their absolute conviction toward their beliefs and their steadfast commitment to positive social change, social justice, and peace further shaped my spirit and lit my passion on fire to be a positive force for humanity that has continued throughout my life. Paradoxically, as I sit here today, with my life having come full circle, I am helping to found a nonprofit organization committed to global social change, social justice, and peace.

Many seminal events in my life helped inform the eventual construction of my life mission to assist individuals and organizations to maximize their potentialities. Many of those events centered around seeing myriad media images of lynching, the wanton murder of people of color around the world, and hearing my father's stories about growing up in Alabama where lynching was a common practice; my Sicilian mother's stories of being abandoned by her family after marrying my father, who was African American, Choctaw, and Creek during a time when many states still had anti-miscegenation laws on their books; my thirst for history; my own experiences engaging racism directly; and watching my son having to do the same. The fact that all of my family members devoured information fostered in me a voracious appetite for consuming information and learning new things and added to my deep desire to make a difference in the lives of others.

A major turning point in my life occurred when I entered college. My formal postsecondary education began at Merritt Jr. College in Oakland, California, which was known as the home of the Black Panther Party. After getting out of the Navy, I transferred to Laney Jr. College, where I obtained my associate of arts degree. My teachers at Laney Jr. College had a profound impact on shaping my belief systems about living my life as an agent of change. I was taught by radical teachers who ensured their students read the likes of Franz Fanon, Paulo Freire, Lerone Bennett, Jr., and Malcom X. These authors, and others like them, further fueled my passion to serve humanity in a meaningful way, provided a framework for the types of employment choices I engaged, and fashioned the manner in which I worked as a practitioner. As a result, Laney Jr. College became my incubator in which I tested my ideas in an academic laboratory and in a way that I was not able to do previously.

By the time I transferred from Laney Jr. College to enroll at San Francisco State, I was in my mid-20s, and I graduated with a degree in social science with a research emphasis.

My coursework taught me to draw upon all of the sciences to do my life's work, whatever that might become. That part of my formal training became the underpinning for my ability to conduct research throughout my career as a scholar-practitioner and framed my skill sets when I began to prepare to complete my dissertation.

During that time, the Vietnam War had just ended, and civil rights efforts were still in full swing. San Francisco State was a rebellious place and the first university to install a Black Studies department. Had someone asked me then whether I would obtain a doctoral degree of any sort during my lifetime, I would have told them no, absolutely not, because I thought that doctors of any ilk were arrogant and certainly not an assemblage that I would ever want to join.

My academic training at that point in time gave me a solid foundation upon which to build the early stages of my professional career as a mid-level executive leader. I had sufficient academic training to sustain my efforts to break barriers in my corporate environment and to fend off arguments against the things I felt were morally and ethically right but that others maintained were not part of the status quo. Although I was never recognized for any of my achievements, I also had the technical capacity to consistently outperform my peers in every category of performance. During the next 10 years or so, I completed as many professional certifications as I could obtain because I endeavored to become the consummate professional. I even became certified as a senior director with a global nonprofit corporation and functioned as a member of its national training staff where I trained other professionals in the organization.

One day, a flier landed on my desk for a master of nonprofit administration (MNA) degree program offered through the University of San Francisco. As one of only a handful of minority employees, my supervisors and peers expended lots of energy trying to convince me that I did not know what I was talking about in my capacity as an executive leader, despite my many operational successes and certifications. I thought by getting my MNA, I would prove to myself and demonstrate to them that I had been right in my thinking all along. However, what I learned in the process was that I became a bigger threat than ever because nearly all of my supervisors and peers had less education and less professional training than I did by the time I graduated.

During many lonely moments, my situation caused me to reflect back to earlier years and how many of my teachers in junior and senior high school tried very hard to convince me that I was inadequate and that I would never become a success. I thought back to my high school counselor, who had only known me for three semesters, yet he told me that I should not even think about going to college, because I would never make it through to getting a degree. Therefore, the dynamics of my life during my mid-career became ever more painful years that were piling on to what already had been a life filled with pain.

Attending the University of San Francisco, which is a Jesuit institution of learning, changed my life in ways that I am still trying to understand. During one of my statistics classes, the teacher announced if we ever thought about getting a doctorate, they had very good programs there. That night changed my life forever. During our break, I went upstairs to the doctoral studies offices that were empty because it was nighttime. I located the brochures for the various programs and took them home for review. When I got home, I looked at each of the brochures and when I read the one about the organization and leadership doctorate, my heart started palpitating vigorously, because it resonated very deeply within me. I knew that it was the program for me and that somehow I would be transformed in ways that I could not understand at the time. That night was the first time in my life that I flipped my internal switch and considered obtaining my doctorate, and I knew in that moment with absolute certainty that I needed to enroll in the organization and leadership doctoral program.

A few days later, I contacted the program chairperson, who did everything he could to convince me that it was not the right program for me and that I should not apply to the University of San Francisco for my doctoral studies. After I completed my MNA courses, I decided to apply to the program, despite the chairperson's efforts to convince me otherwise. About a third of the way through my doctoral program, I was sitting in my favorite professor's office, and a man passed by his office space. He turned to me and asked me if I knew who that person was, and I said no. He said, he used to be the chairperson of the program, and he tried to keep you out of the program. He went on to tell me that he took great pleasure in telling the former chairperson that I was one of the best students they had in the program when he asked why I was admitted into the program.

As I think about that exchange, I have mixed emotions about it. On the one hand, I see my life as being a series of efforts to prove myself to those whom I have come to consider as people who feel the need to discount my accomplishments in order for them to feel better about themselves. On the other hand, I am grateful to them for inspiring me to prove them wrong, and in the meantime, forcing me to work harder to outperform them in every way possible, thereby helping me to become a highly skilled scholar-practitioner.

My doctoral journey has been one of deep passion for my chosen subject matter. It has been a journey of shaping my truth as a scholar-practitioner engaged as an agent of transformation within whatever environments I find myself performing. Most importantly, it has been a journey to find my peace as a being with value. Although I have come to know how much I do not know about my area of study and about life itself, I have also developed the confidence and technical expertise to shape what I believe to be truth within my areas of expertise and interests. I have established the technical competence to create knowledge and new ways of thinking about problems. I have learned to leverage my doctorate to bring about effective change in the lives of the individuals and organizations with whom I work, and I am using my training to create social change, social justice, and peace for myself and for others.

My doctorate has opened doors that would have otherwise been closed had it not been obtained, and when necessary, it has given me the wherewithal to go head-to-head with anyone I encounter. Despite all of these things, I do not see myself as an extraordinary person. However, I do see myself as an ordinary person who has simply chosen to have extraordinary dreams for creating a world that is very different from the one that I have encountered during my lifelong journey to become who I am today. Thanks to the many lessons learned along that journey, my passion is to live a life in service to others with no other desire than to leave no footprints or fingerprints on my work. My truth is to strive to find the hope in hopeless, the possible in the impossible, and the best in all whom I encounter. My peace comes in knowing that I have an insatiable appetite for learning and that the mastery of anything is a lifelong process of working toward perfection, yet never achieving it, because there is always something new to learn. Therefore, I will never be bored with life or have my appetite fulfilled. In that regard, as I live my life with the end in mind, there is nothing more I can ask from a life well lived.

10
Annie Brown, PhD

Educator, Author, and Owner/Chief Executive Officer AnnBro International Training and Business Consulting, LLC

My Purpose for Living

I am on this earth to make a positive social impact by serving with honesty, integrity, and sincerity. I go the extra mile to help others.

The Beginning

I am a doctor, but my journey was not easy. As with other newborn infants, I entered this world with no knowledge of who I was. I had no idea about my purpose for living. I did not even know the meaning of purpose. As I matured, step-by-step, I discovered I had a mother and a father and numerous other close relatives who loved me. My dad was a military man, and my mom was a loving housewife. My seven siblings and I experienced much joy and happiness. I do not remember any sadness from age 0 to 5. Then, I had a life-changing experience. One morning, 2 days prior to my sixth birthday, I heard my dad crying. My mother had died in her sleep. I did not really understand death, and I do not remember much about the events during that time period, but sadness crept in. My youngest brother was a preemie and only 6 weeks old. Now what?

As best I can remember, my mother's parents did not give my dad an option. They insisted we move in with them. Yes, all nine of us. My grandparents had 14 children. Two were deceased, including my mom. At least half of my grandparents' children were still living at home, with the youngest being only nine. Yet, what options did my dad really have—a man in his early thirties with eight children. So, my grandparents became our parents. My dad even called them Ma and Pa. Later, I heard my mother/grandmother say she had to have all of us raised in the same household with the same values. I grew up in a value system based on God first and much love.

Some people may have panicked to have such a large family with presumably numerous economic challenges. I was raised with much faith, love, and prayers because my siblings, including my extended siblings, did not experience the lack that someone may expect. Certainly, we had family challenges, but my reasoning is based on the following facts: we had love, we had a warm place to stay, we had beds, we had food to eat, we had a car to ride in, we went to school, we had books, we had clothes to wear, we went to church every Sunday, we had lots of people at our home on Sunday, we went to the movies, and we attended school events. Even though I had a lot of fun as a child, reality hit just before I entered sixth grade.

I was 11 years old and on summer vacation in New York, having traveled from South Carolina. I loved spending summers in New York. Five of my extended family members and their spouses lived in New York. My father and parents/grandparents would only allow some of their children to stay temporarily with immediate family during summer months. My parents were extremely protective. I was elated that they trusted me enough to allow me go for the summer. Even though Coney Island, Rockaway Beach, the donuts on Jamaica Avenue, and the hotdogs in Manhattan were highlights and fascinating, I had the opportunity to attend the World's Fair. I was spellbound. I could not have imagined what my eyes would behold.

At the World's Fair, I was amazed at the amount of innovation, especially with technology. I felt as if I was in a different world. I saw diverse groups of people of all nationalities. I was captivated by what I saw and the many lessons I learned. The innovators of the World's Fair were making a social impact by sharing information in a forum that promoted learning in an interesting and remarkable manner. The universal themes had a major impact on me. I decided during that summer that I was going to get as much education as I could because I wanted to know as much as I could about the world.

Educational Journey

My parents taught me that a wise man will hear and will increase learning (Proverb 1:5). They ensured that my siblings and I went to school every day, unless we were severely ill. I did not want to miss any days because I did not want to miss any new lessons. I was passionate about learning.

When I was in secondary school, I had two goals. I wanted to be valedictorian, and I aspired to be a math or English teacher. I was successful at becoming valedictorian, but an academic counselor convinced me that I would be an excellent computer programmer. I took the advice and deferred my goal of being a teacher. I am still amazed that the counselor did not advocate teaching. I deduced the counselor wanted me to be on the cutting edge of computer technology because I was obsessive about math. I chose to attend a community college because the college had a rigorous computer technology program (formerly data processing). I was fascinated with the intricacies of computers and with computer programming. I challenged myself to become one of the best programmers in a male-dominated industry.

I consistently chose to take the road less traveled because I was inspired by Robert Frost's poem, *The Road Not Taken*. I learned the poem in middle school. I interpreted the poem to mean I had choices, and I had no plans to compromise the goals I knew I could obtain regardless of the challenges. In my quest for an associate degree in computer technology, I was initially the only minority and one of two females in my class. Later, I was enrolled in an undergraduate program at a college where many learners had difficulty graduating because of the rigorous academic programs. All my professors were male except one. I had no minority professors. The same was true for graduate school. My professors were supportive and encouraging, even though the program was rigorous and I would not compromise my other priorities: wife, mom, full-time employee, and church and community worker. I sacrificed sleep. I do not advise others to mimic my actions because I was obsessive about being all things to all people and about learning. I performed admirably in my classes because I viewed every class I took as an opportunity to learn more. The more I learned, the more I wanted to learn.

After obtaining, a bachelor of business administration in management with a cognate in English, I earned a master of business administration. I thought I had self-actualized. I had a family I adored and a job in information management that I was passionate about. I was able to qualify for a job at the community college I attended because of my degree in computer technology. Actually, I did not have to apply for the job. My computer technology professor requested I take the job less than 1 month after obtaining my associate degree. I was instrumental in establishing the organized information processing department at the college. I performed at a very high level. I was the catalyst for organized computer training at the college. I excelled at helping other leaders in the college establish a user-friendly information processing system. The executive leaders at my college eventually gave me the opportunity to establish a formal training program for all administrators, faculty, and staff. I represented the college throughout the community. I advocated education, and I was a positive voice for the college and the community served.

While serving in the community, at national training events, and in other educational arenas, I began to hear more about doctoral degrees. I met individuals who took much pride in being a member of a minute population of people who held a doctoral degree. According to the U.S. Census in 2000, only 1% of individuals earned a doctoral degree, specifically a Ph.D. I became obsessed with the knowledge that the doctoral degree was the highest degree in my field. I decided I had to have a PhD so that I could self-actualize.

I always challenged myself, and I took much pride in taking the road less traveled. No one in my immediate family had earned a doctoral degree. I did not ask why I should put that much pressure on myself. Instead, I asked why I shouldn't. I concluded I had no valid reason to deny myself the opportunity to increase my education to a level where I could do a greater good by helping more people. The doctoral program challenged me immensely, but I did not waiver. The day I defended my dissertation was one of the most stressful days of my life, but the reward was worth the pain.

My Influence

If I can help someone as I journey on my way, my living is not in vain.
—Anonymous

I have to meditate and pray frequently. When I was growing up, prayer was not an option in my home, it was a welcomed habit. I treat people the way I want to be treated. Even though I had a lot of book knowledge, my mother/grandmother had a lot of wisdom. She taught me to ask the following questions before making a comment about an individual: Is it kind? Is it true? She said even if a statement is true, do not repeat it if it is unkind. I continue to take that lesson with me into my classroom and training sessions. I encourage others to overcome obstacles. One of my favorite sayings is with every negative there is a greater positive. I am an extreme optimist who cringes when I hear the word *can't*.

I am still amazed that I am a member of an elite group of individuals. While the number of individuals holding a doctoral degree has increased since I was awarded my degree, the statistics for doctoral earners are still low. According to the U.S. Census in 2013, less than 1.68% of Americans over the age of 25 have earned a PhD, with only 4% of all PhD holders being Afro-American. This equates to approximately 2.5 million people. People with professional degrees such as an MD or DDS make up 1.48% of the U.S. population, which makes the total percentage of Americans referred to as doctors equal to 3.16%.

I later became a faculty member at my community college, and I currently teach in two doctoral programs. I am a lifelong learner and an infinite teacher. My dream was deferred, but it was not denied. As I teach and meet others, I motivate them to take full advantage of the opportunity to learn. I have mentored numerous learners in undergraduate and doctoral programs. I coauthored the eighth volume of *The Refractive Thinker*, and I began a real estate company to help others resolve their real estate needs.

Because of my character, education, and working knowledge, I have earned the respect of others I serve. I have been instrumental in helping to establish educational and nonprofit organizations. I take pride in the work I did with a local Chamber of Commerce to establish a cultural diversity program, Building Bridges, in southeastern South Carolina. I have done a lot to promote economic diversity.

Lessons I Have learned

As an educator and motivator speaker, I continue to operate on the basic principle established by parents in my youth: the golden rule. As learning increased, I enhanced my knowledge by adopting other relevant principles to live by. I begin with the end in mind, and I seek first to understand, then to be understood (Covey, 1989).

I often concentrate on the words of Mahatma Gandhi: Be the Change you want to see in the world. I know that if it is to be, it is up to me to do all I can to make this world a better place to live and work. Education is the key. Martin Luther King, Jr. said the purpose of education is to teach one to think and to think critically. I will not let my education be in vain. I have learned to listen, to think, and to share.

My Contributions to Social Change

In addition to working with the Chamber of Commerce to develop a cultural diversity program, I worked with the Chamber on leadership development programs and the

Downtown Development Board to revitalize the downtown area in my region. I am active on church and community boards such as the United Way, Hospice, and the School Foundation Board where lives are being changed through grants and school readiness initiatives. I continue to volunteer because of my unyielding desire to serve.

I have assisted numerous learners in their quest to learn and to obtain their doctoral degrees. Some of the learners I mentored are making a social impact by consulting in health and educational arenas. I consistently advise learners to be positive contributors to society.

I am committed to honesty, integrity, and sincerity without compromise. The road to my PhD was not easy, but it was a road I had to take. I am glad I had the wisdom to take the road less traveled, and that has made all the difference. I am operating in my purpose. I look in the mirror, and I love the person I see.

Reference

Covey, S. R. (1989). *The 7 habits of highly effective people*. New York, NY: Fireside.

11
Tom Butkiewicz, PhD

Educator

All I do as a contributing faculty member at Walden University is tailored to help doctoral learners become inspired, energized, and empowered by his/her purpose and passion in life on the road to positive social change.
—Tom Butkiewicz

Passion is the ultimate energizer for your purpose in life. Organizational leaders would benefit by realizing that passion is what fuels that journey and serves as the driving force to help employees grow and reach their destiny. No matter how majestic the dream of a leader, if others do not see the possibility of realizing their hopes and dreams, they will not follow. Without passion, individuals usually become complacent, and complacency leads to unfulfilled dreams. Passion unleashes intrinsic motivation for persons to become enthused about deploying their strengths with meaning and purpose. Energy dispels from persons working in their strength zone, as they are consumed with the notion that once their work is complete, the outcome is joy, excitement, and a sense of fulfillment. A person with passion often exceeds expectations in the workplace. The quantity of the work, however, is not the driving force. The point is that leaders with passion and purpose attract kindred spirits as followers so they can achieve their goals. If leaders need one core competency, it is the ability to sense purpose and passion in others. Leaders can build relationships over time by genuinely knowing their followers, listening to them, and expressing appreciation for their contributions at work.

Purpose and passion are mutually reinforcing for leaders to build structures of understanding geared toward what matters most to others. Leaders should reframe their thinking by concentrating on how to serve others the way they desire to be served. A common thread is the starting point that forms a pattern of human needs into a medley by which leaders can transform organizations to become conduits for positive social change. I influence change around me by expressing sincere interest in others at work by engaging in conversation about what is most important to them. Listening carefully brings a sense of what people want, what they value, what motivates them to do their best work, and what their hopes are in navigating the journey of life.

Pessimists typically hold limiting beliefs. The doubts of fear and failure that are natural to individuals striving to achieve something great become internalized and ossify there, creating friction and dissonance while containing hope that can unleash when filled with belief. Great leaders create hope, not just financial stability. The values of freedom, community diversity, and social change responsibility attract people to a common cause that lead to a life of significance. Leaders should have a determination to make a difference in the world. The pursuit of significance in life requires a personal and professional transformation. A disposition toward serving others is necessary to improve lives. Successful transformational leaders should always measure their efforts in service of a better world. I embrace and practice transformational leadership by illuminating the path for others to see a brighter future. Transformational leaders not only show the way but also are the first to begin creating the path for others to follow. My intention is to create a disposition with principles that leads beyond the immediate and mundane on the quest from ordinary to extraordinary. If leaders can achieve significance in this way, then, and only then, they can serve others in activities that influence positive social change.

Success is the significance you attract by the person you become in a personal and professional way. The transition from ordinary to extraordinary occurs when individuals pursue something greater than themselves. The measures of success for leaders signify the value of their passage through life. The most important principles to make the shift from ordinary to extraordinary are purpose, hope, and determination. Most individuals want to know there is purpose to their existence. The workplace may offer that purpose for persons who locate a place where they seek hope for a better future. Exemplary leaders have the determination to draw out and make use of the human desire for meaning and fulfillment by communicating how each person is part of something larger than what can be seen in the present. The future is just not some place the leaders and followers are going to, but a place they are creating. Leaders elevate the human spirit by uncovering what employees care about individually, as a group, and as a company. Even the most inspirational people cannot transition from ordinary to extraordinary unless they, as leaders and followers, work together despite any obstacles or personal agendas. Uniting with a mutual cause brings individuals together in purpose, hope, and determination that result in a life of meaning and purpose. Leaders must show others how they will be served and how their unique needs can be satisfied.

Mastering strategies for removing obstacles to become organized allowed me to focus on who I am and what is crucial as a doctoral degree holder. Effective organizing forced me to view an enlarged territory, not just for an ordinary life but also to effect extraordinary change in the world. Dr. Walter McCollum, a Fulbright Scholar and my faculty chair, provided consultations on preparing to become a scholar-practitioner. The lessons learned on my doctoral journey included, but were not limited to, applying effective time management best practices, publishing scholarly peer-reviewed articles, presenting at academic conferences, and making a difference by strategically thinking, acting, and influencing others to impact positive social change.

While the past is the prologue, the present is the opportunity. The past comes with knowledge and experience from which to draw. The present brings about a level of change with the possibility to apply knowledge and experience from my doctoral journey. Gazing into the past helps lengthen the future with purpose, hope, and determination. My purpose and hope were to become a contributing faculty member teaching in the PhD in Management program at Walden University. Successful leaders have high standards, both of themselves and of their colleagues. These expectations are powerful, as they are frames into which people fit reality. Dr. McCollum is a scholar-practitioner with high standards of himself and of those persons in his sphere of influence. My dream became reality when Dr. McCollum helped fulfill my purpose and hope to become a contributing faculty member teaching in the PhD in Management program at Walden University. As a contributing faculty member, I am committed to impacting the level of change in each doctoral student so he or she is adequately prepared for a transition from ordinary to extraordinary. Being student-centered brings about diverse opportunities to inspire, energize, and empower doctoral students to create a path for a future that involves making a key difference in the world through positive social change.

Making a transition from ordinary to extraordinary would have been impossible if it were not for extraordinary people in my life. My first debt of gratitude goes to my faculty chair and now colleague, Dr. McCollum, who provided scholarly support and meaningful encouragement throughout the dissertation process and beyond. Dr. McCollum shared his knowledge and wisdom so I could become a scholar-practitioner equipped to effect social change. His thoughtful insights enabled me to create a new path for the future with direction toward a purposeful life serving others. I was blessed that God sent Dr. McCollum to guide me on this educational journey.

The unwavering sacrifices my family made far exceeded my expectations, which make these special thanks heartfelt. I would like to thank my wife, Debi, for her endless love by sharing in my passion to achieve this lifelong goal. To my son, Tom, for his love that motivated me to earn this terminal degree despite some unforeseen challenges along the way. I am also grateful to my parents and family for their love and believing in me to be successful in life. My mother is beaming from heaven above, knowing my dissertation was in her honor and that she left a legacy for future generations.

God gave me the gifts to make my lifelong goal a reality. What I do with these gifts becomes my gift to God. I am humbled by the opportunity to go beyond my limits with these gifts so what seems impossible becomes possible by the grace of God. I pray that my wife, son, parents, family, and Dr. McCollum enjoy an abundance of blessings.

12
Charles Senteio, PhD, MBA, MSW

Educator
President and CEO, Namamai Services, LLC

My Ongoing Journey from Success to Significance

Growth and comfort rarely occupy the same place at the same time. Embrace the grind in pursuit of higher ground.

The day I stop giving is the day I stop receiving. The day I stop learning is the day I stop growing.
—Unknown

Purpose and passion have always been central to my academic, professional, and personal pursuits. My parents instilled the deep importance of finding what I now call significance in my life's journey. They both began their careers as public school educators. My mother spent her entire career as a third-grade teacher; my father taught at the secondary level and retired as a superintendent. I had a good sense of what my mother did as a grade school teacher, reinforced by her insistence that my schoolwork must satisfy her, even when my teachers gave me the maximum amount of gold stars. My father was an administrator by the time I reached adolescence, so although I realized that their work was quite different, I also witnessed that both of my parents approached their work with passion and meaning. Of course, they faced the persistent challenges about which almost anyone remotely familiar with primary and secondary public education is well aware, but their passion for education was persistent. Although my parents are retired, I still get a front row view of these challenges as my sister, and only sibling, is a guidance counselor in a public high school. Public education is not among my varied professional activities, but the people closest to me who were educators worked with passion and purpose rooted in service. I simply never knew, or wanted to know, a career that did not afford me the same set of privileges.

My purpose has certainly evolved over the course of the 25 years since I completed my undergraduate degree in mathematics and computer science. Like most undergraduates, I did not have the autonomy I desired in my career and educational options. I simply took advantage of the opportunities I was fortunate enough to have access to. I worked as a programmer/systems analyst during my last few years of college and that experience taught me how critical it was to have options. I enjoyed programming but I did not have a passion for it, at least not the passion I felt was necessary for me to feel fulfilled in a career. I did, however, have considerable passion for generating career options. This was the main reason I decided to pursue an MBA. At the time, no one in my network had earned an MBA. But my good friend's girlfriend had gone to business school. When I asked her about her MBA, she confirmed that someone like me—who had never taken a business course—could be accepted to business school, so I decided to go to the best program I could get admitted to. I left the Northeast where I grew up to attend the Ross School of Business at the University of Michigan, in a state where I knew no one and had never visited. My passion for generating options prevailed over any reluctance to embark upon something new. In fact, I was energized by the challenge. It turned out to be a terrific decision. I greatly expanded my network and generated options.

Upon graduation from business school, I again decided to embark upon something new. I was fortunate to have several career options and chose to accept a position as a strategy consultant based in Dallas. This was work for which I had little background and again in a state I had never visited. I did this work for close to 10 years; I enjoyed it, but I did not feel moved by it. The work was wonderfully challenging. I had the opportunity to work and visit six continents, leading projects across the United States, Europe, and Asia. I had the opportunity to influence strategic design across several industries by working closely with a wide variety of senior executives. I began to both understand my own purpose and realize that this work was not aligned with that purpose. This became increasingly clear in the course of my philanthropic activities. I found considerable fulfillment in attempting to address the vexing challenges in my role as board chair for a south Dallas nonprofit organization that supported those affected by HIV, incarceration, and violence. At that point, my purpose was evolving from just generating options to generating options that might get me closer to understanding, and to some degree defining, my purpose. I was not sure that selling and managing international IT strategy engagements would accomplish this. This was when I first started thinking deeply about the journey toward purpose in what became a necessary progression from success to significance. My varied and international experiences taught me that not all successful people are significant, but all significant people are successful.

I left strategy consulting to focus on finding my purpose and to chase significance. I had a very clear epiphany. I would continue my journey to begin a new one by focusing on health care. Again, this was an industry I knew very little about, and one in which I had a very limited network. However, I did know that health care touched everyone at some point in his or her life. I thought I could find opportunities to impact lives in a more meaningful way. I was not clear on what role, job, or specific area of health care I would pursue. I was also not at all interested in "finding myself" by unplugging from a daily routine to go away and think about what I wanted to do. Perhaps that would have been a better, or at least a more thoughtful, approach. I am simply too restless for that; from a financial perspective, I did not need to work immediately, but I knew I wanted to find something that might more closely align to my purpose. Tavis Smiley stated what Maya Angelou shared with him shortly before she passed away: "People find their path by walking it" (Stewart, 2015). I did not want to just walk; I wanted to run!

Value of Relationships

We are inevitably our brother's keeper because we are our brother's brother. What affects one directly affects us all indirectly.
—Rev. Dr. Martin Luther King, Jr.

For as long as I can recall, I have enjoyed and seen the value in the continuous process of getting to know people and embracing them getting to know me. The process of developing and nurturing relationships—personal, professional, and the vast spectrum in between—remains intriguing, and this interest served me well as I started my adventure into health care. I reached out to the only person I knew who worked in health care. At the time, Eric was a fellow board member who worked for a large hospital. He introduced me to Sam, his mentor, a physician and hospital executive who actually dissuaded me from becoming a physician, which was my goal at the time. This goal was borne of being fairly uninformed about how I could leverage my skills and experience to support health and wellness, which of course Sam recognized immediately. Sam encouraged me to seek ways to apply my business strategy expertise to follow my interest in addressing health care disparities experienced by vulnerable patient populations.

Once he realized my stubbornness, which I like to spin as "dogged determination," Sam did two wonderful things for me; the second would greatly influence my trajectory. First, he encouraged me to pursue training as an emergency medical technician (EMT). He thought that understanding health care delivery at that level would offer me rich insights. Second, he recommended I meet Jim, another physician and health care executive who, unlike Sam, still saw patients. I met Jim and, once I finished my EMT training, I started hanging out with him as he saw patients for a half day a week at a free clinic and doing home visits.

Doing hundreds of home visits with Jim broadened my appreciation for the complexities associated with health care delivery. I began to refine my understanding of the confluence of factors that influence why some patients seem to suffer disparate outcomes, including social determinates, health behavior, health policy, environmental health, and informatics capabilities. This relationship quickly led to consulting engagements and research projects focused on both the business and the clinical aspects of health care delivery. As my network expanded, I tried to learn as much as I could about the various issues that impacted health and about myself. I was beginning to get some clarity on purpose and what making a difference might mean for me. I was extremely energized by the people in my growing health network who encouraged me to leverage my previous business acumen to quantify and communicate the value of charity care and help develop sustainable efforts that seemed to make a difference. For example, I saw that performing home visits for vulnerable patients resulted in business value while avoiding hospital admissions. When I picked health care—or perhaps when health care picked me—I had absolutely no presupposition that my previous academic or professional experience would be relevant or interesting to the people I would meet. I was glad to learn that it was not just interesting but also valuable. My relationships were grounded in reciprocity. Although I did not have experience in health care, I had experience recognizing the factors that influenced complex issues and developing approaches to improve them. I was contributing meaningfully to these activities and learning a great deal.

Working closely with researchers gave me the opportunity to begin to understand what research was and what role it could have in my journey. Participating on various health disparities project teams connected me with scholars from various fields, such as sociology, epidemiology, medicine, medical anthropology, and social work. I also read a lot; after all, I had much to learn.

A life is not important except in the impact it has on others' lives.
　　　　　—Appears on Jackie Robinson's gravestone at Cypress Hills Cemetery in Brooklyn

Two books stand out. First, *Mountains Beyond Mountains* outlines the journey of Dr. Paul Farmer, who continues to fight inequity and injustice. This work gave me a global perspective on structural issues that influence population health outcomes. This resonated because I saw parallels with my international business experience. It also showed me what a profound impact an individual can have in addressing health disparities on a global scale.

Ask not what disease the patient has, ask what patient the disease has.
　　　　　　　　　　　　　　　　　—Sir William Osler

The Spirit Catches You and You Fall Down is the other. It is a compelling story told from a social worker's perspective about how all the advantages of modern, Western medicine still have a way to go to understand the rich nuances of individuals who may view medications and other recommended treatments differently. The book traces the experiences of Hmong immigrants as they attempted to navigate the U.S. health care system and reinforces the important lesson that we can all learn from those who have different backgrounds than ourselves.

After building a health services company with a consulting practice, which I expanded to home health and hospice services, I began to contemplate that my purpose might need to expand further. I was enjoying my work—which also included teaching a health class in a Texas state jail and serving as an adjunct instructor in a school of nursing and teaching mathematics—but I was frustrated with my inability to affect change on a broader level. The researchers I was working with suggested I consider pursuing a PhD so that I could define my own projects. After some brief reflection, I agreed with them and decided to go back to school for my doctorate. I thought the skills I could develop and the credentials would grant me access to opportunities I did not have. My rationale was very similar to my other decisions, but it became more precise; I wanted to increase my options in pursuit of higher ground.

Expanding Universe

Before going back to college, I knew I didn't want to be an intellectual, spending my life in books and libraries without knowing what the hell is going on in the streets. Theory

without practice is just as incomplete as practice without theory. The two have to go together
—Assata Shakur

I have always been interested in enacting change. As I learned more about health care, I became very interested in psychosocial factors—the individual and environmental factors that influence health. My doctoral studies in health informatics enabled me to further understand the ways in which psychological and social factors (i.e., life stressors, level of social support, financial barriers) impact self-care behavior (Senteio, 2015). In my dissertation project, I detailed how these factors impact diabetes outcomes and built upon the literature to describe how health care practitioners—physicians, nurses, pharmacists, and diabetes educators—access and use this information as they care for diabetes patients.

My territory has expanded in several areas as a result of my doctoral study. First, I understand and consequently appreciate the impact of research. For example, although I had worked with medical anthropologists and public health researchers in my philanthropic and consulting work, I never actually dug in to understand what research was and, more importantly, how I could use it to help others in pursuit of my own significance. *Mountains Beyond*

Mountains furthered my understanding of the complex issues that public health and medical practitioners face. *The Spirit Catches You and Falls Down* gave me a better sense of what social workers and medical anthropologists study in identifying where our current health care system needs improvement. So, while reading books informed my purpose, my doctoral studies helped to refine my understanding of how this work could fit into my own journey. In my doctoral classes, I learned much of the history and evolution of information science. For example, Simon's influential work, *The Science of the Artificial*, helped me see the links between psychology and engineering design. These linkages will be important as I develop improved health informatics tools to collect and use psychosocial information. Second, although I have just embarked on my career as a health care researcher, I have already had the opportunity to continue to shape my research agenda. For example, in my second year of my doctoral program, I was a research assistant supporting a project to investigate the experience of African American patients from poor urban areas with multiple chronic diseases. I asked one of the participants why he was not on the transplant list, since going to dialysis was such a burden for him. His response struck me: "Charles, you know we

Black folks don't get kidneys." Recently I was awarded a seed grant to investigate why some chronic kidney disease patients elect to not be put on, or choose to be removed from, the kidney transplant list, despite this being the recommended regimen for those eligible for transplant. This is representative of how I am now actively shaping work that supports my three areas of health research:

1. *evaluation* of current health care capabilities,
2. *identification* of areas of improvement, and
3. *development* of new capabilities and *measurement* of their impact.

My research agenda has been in development for more than a decade now and was shaped well prior to my doctoral study through my philanthropic and entrepreneurial activities. I continue to integrate my experiences as a consultant, entrepreneur, and scholar. My universe is expanding, and I hope it continues to.

Key Principles

In school, you're taught a lesson and then given a test. In life, you're given a test that teaches you a lesson.
—Tom Bodett

I have never embraced a long-term career plan. I recall in sixth grade I had an assignment to write an essay on what I wanted to be when I grew up. I did not have a clue. I knew I wanted to have the opportunity to do whatever I set my mind to. My parents instilled the notion that I could achieve anything with requisite work and enthusiasm. I still tell them that I remain naive enough to continue believing just that. I eschew a long-term plan because I think it limits me. In my current mentoring relationships, I have observed a pressure to insist that our young people determine "what they want to do with their lives." I think this places unnecessary and pointless pressure on them. I encourage them to generate options, instead of wrestling to make this kind of decision.

When I first entered health care, I never thought of going back to school. In fact, I was in my mid-30s before I discovered that health care—an industry I had never worked in or thought about working in—might be part of my path. I have found it particularly useful to embrace the unknown. It has been very important for me to remain flexible; pliability is perhaps one of the key attributes in the pursuit of passion. Remaining grounded in key goals while remaining flexible in where the journey can take you can be a delicate balance to strike, but continues to be essential as I continue my journey. I am energized by tackling difficult, new challenges. I currently focus on improving how health care practitioners and patients can use information to make more informed decisions that result in improved chronic disease outcomes. This is a tall problem and a tremendous opportunity. I'd be selling myself short by being too narrow, too convinced, too sure, too rigid. When I first began my journey in health care, I ran across a very accomplished orthopedic surgeon who shared, "The more I learn the less I'm sure." Now I find myself referring to the literature to understand what is known about a topic so I can work out what still needs to be understood. Developing research skills has armed me with more tools to evaluate thoughtfully where I'll invest my time, resources, and network in pursuit of "higher ground." These endeavors demand flexibility that can result in discomfort, which is to be expected, as growth and comfort rarely occupy the same place at the same time.

Key Lessons

The following key lessons have helped me on my path: (a) strive to have good problems, (b) embrace the discomfort necessary for higher ground, (c) keep the faith by walking it and by cultivating relationships, and (d) try to enjoy the journey.

Be regular and orderly in your life, so that you may be violent and original in your work.
—Gustave Flaubert

I have learned that we all have problems, so it is folly to try to eliminate them. I try to ensure I have good problems. For example, having to decide between two good job offers is a good problem. But not having a job and not knowing where to begin to look for one is a bad problem. Explaining the steps necessary to renew your passport to try and convince your mom that renewing hers will not be a big hassle is a good problem. But explaining to your mom you cannot renew your passport because you owe child support is a bad problem. I actually like having good problems, because I know my resources are finite. After all, we only have a finite amount of time and emotional energy to expend. I try to focus my energies on challenges that will support my own endeavors and those of others. Therefore, having good problems is not so bad.

I try to consider challenges as opportunities. Returning to school reinforced my perspective on the importance of learning and the value in connecting previous lessons. My social work training forced me to take a closer look at myself through learning about the experiences of others.

Along the way, I learned more about my own opportunities to grow and develop.

Superlative performance is really a confluence of dozens of small skills or activities, each one learned or stumbled upon, which have been carefully drilled into habit and then are fitted together in a synthesized whole.
—Daniel Chambliss

Learning and applying knowledge has always been interesting and fun, but the process of acquiring it is laborious and what Chambliss calls "mundane." The pursuit of larger goals inevitably comes with drudgery associated with the daily grind. Embracing the grind enables the larger goals. Indeed, growth and comfort rarely occupy the same place at the same time, and the grind can certainly be uncomfortable. But it is a worthwhile toll to pay en route to higher ground, and for me that price is overshadowed by the daunting possibility of not being a good steward of the many blessings I have been given.

Those who have a 'why' to live, can bear with almost any 'how.'
—Viktor Frankl

My journey in health care continues as a researcher, instructor, and entrepreneur. It has been characterized by my attempts to move toward that purpose seeking that "higher ground." This sentiment is captured beautifully in this excerpt from Johnson Oatman Jr.'s hymn "Let Us Go Up to the Mountain of the Lord."

I'm pressing on the upward way, New heights I'm gaining every day;
Still praying as I'm onward bound, "Lord, plant my feet on higher ground."

Hope is fundamental to my faith and indispensable in my pursuit of higher ground. Hope helps sustain the journey, which at times can be arduous. I have been very fortunate to have a family who has always been supportive; I certainly did a good job of picking my parents. I also have an expanding network of people with whom I share very special bonds, grounded in reciprocity. But there certainly have been difficult times and occasions when I was uncertain about how things might turn out in my quest for "significance."

When human wisdom cannot see a hand's breadth before it in the dark night of suffering, then faith can see God, for faith sees best in the dark.
—Soren Kierkegarrd

Chasing "significance," an admittedly nebulous goal, is risky. Failure is undoubtedly a possibility, so faith helps to maintain hope and fierce optimism, which both fuel the fire that helps sustain us through the inevitable difficult times. For me, relationships and faith have been integrated for a very long time. John F. Kennedy said in concluding his inauguration speech, "Here on earth God's work must truly be our own." I attempt to walk my faith through my relationships, deeply rooted in reciprocity, which is necessary to sustain them. They enable me to do my work. They help uplift me, and are undoubtedly my most precious assets; they are unique, dynamic, and irreplaceable.

Little do ye know your own blessedness; for to travel hopefully is a better thing than to arrive, and the true success is to labour.
—Robert Louis Stevenson

I have read and listened to the notion that the journey is just as important as the destination. We must stop and smell the roses and appreciate the journey. I understand this in my head, but I have not fully heard it in my heart. This is a lesson I still need to learn.

I thirst but never quench, I know the consequence, feeling as I do.
—"I Write A Song For You," Earth Wind and Fire

I am not one to readily celebrate the journey, and this likely detracts from it. In my own way, I acknowledge victories large and small, but I have yet to truly learn how to do this well. This is an area of growth that is ahead and will no doubt enhance my efficacy in defining and pursuing my higher ground. I look forward to continuing the journey.

13
Dr. Savitri Dixon-Saxon

Dean
School of Counseling and Barbara Solomon
School of Social Work and Human Services
Walden University

A Door Wide Open

I have been living my entire life being prepared as an educator. In my family, there are over 30 educators across three generations. While education is the family business, I did not want it to be my business. I wanted to carve my own path, but I think I am the educator I am today because I was groomed as a child to help other people reach their potential. I was also taught that education could open doors that would be closed without it. I was not just trained to be an educator, but I was groomed to be an educator with a mission toward access and opportunity. In 1969, the prolific singer and songwriter James Brown wrote a song titled "I Don't Want Nobody to Give Me Nothing." The title leads the refrain for the song and is followed by "Open up the door and I'll get it myself." Growing up in a South that was trying to still define desegregation and was actively resistant to integration, I was socialized in a history of closed doors to African Americans and women. But not until I became a divorced custodial parent with limited resources did I understand how single parenthood and poverty impacted access and opportunity. It was during that transition that I learned that you are not meant to go through every closed door, but when a door is opened, you will be prepared going in and coming out of it.

A Defining Moment

Shortly after I received my PhD, I found out that I was going to have child. To those family and friends who knew that I was in a troubled marriage, the timing seemed really bad. Former professors and classmates felt that a child was definitely going to impact those opportunities I had professionally. To support my daughter during the end of my marriage and on, I worked three, sometimes four, jobs that were good jobs, but not exactly enough to make for a fulfilling career. I continued my work as an administrator in student affairs. I worked as an adjunct faculty at two universities in my area. I served in an interim position as an assessment coordinator. I worked full time as a counselor at a university counseling center, and I provided outpatient therapy for an agency in my community serving primarily African American boys. I knew that I wanted to use my degree, but for at least 3 years, it seemed as if I was not going to get a single opportunity that was fulfilling enough and it was difficult for me to leave my support system of family and friends for a better position. More than at any other time in my life, it seemed as if my personal life was impacting my professional opportunities.

Recognizing how tiring and less-than-optimal my work schedule was as a single parent, a friend told me about a part-time teaching opportunity at Walden University that would allow me to supplement my income without having to be away from my daughter so many evenings. I had applied for a position with the university before, but this position in the School of Psychology seemed more closely aligned with my training and education. I was trained in counseling and counselor education, but I had a graduate minor in psychology. I was interviewed by phone for a position at this mysterious distance learning university with one interviewer and six other applicants for the position. I had never been in an interview like that, and even though the interviewer made it clear to us that we were all being considered for several positions, the interview felt much like a dog and pony show. Being the only counselor educator among five other psychologists, I felt much like a mule. I kept going through the interview, realizing how small my teaching niche would be, but determined to keep going forward because I saw it as important to improving my daughter's life. I never tried to pretend that I was a psychologist. I was very clear that I was a counselor educator and I shared my experiences. While it was hard, I refused to be distracted by those others on the call who obviously had so much more experience as psychologists.

At one point in the interview, the interviewer asked me, "Have you ever considered working at Walden full-time? I am looking at your vitae and you have a lot of the experiences we are looking for in a mental health counseling program we are developing." At that moment, I clearly and distinctly heard the voice of God and He said, "Do not close a door." Without knowing much at all about the position, I said, "Yes, I would love to hear more about the position." This moment changed the dynamic of that interview. The other interviewees who had been previously so keen to share their experiences as practitioners and scholars in psychology started making sure the interviewer knew of their counseling and administrative experiences. I realized a good mule can make a good showing even at a dog and pony show.

I have shared some version of this story many times, because it was a defining moment for me. I got the position the interviewer referenced because I had experience in higher education administration, teaching, counseling in various settings, and assessment. When the interviewer shared the job description with me, it was as if they had written the position description with me in mind. I had all of the keys to go through the open door at that moment.

Wisdom: Knowing How to Find the Answers

Many of my professional colleagues thought that it was a risk to skip so many steps professionally to become chair of an academic program. I knew enough about my abilities and work ethic not to think that I was completely out of my depth, but I knew that I needed to assemble the right team. My eighth-grade English teacher, Oliver Caesar Sims, used to tell me, "Dixon, intelligence is not having all of the answers, but knowing where to find the answers."

I know where to go to find the answers. Everything I have been able to accomplish has been the result of identifying the right people for great teams and using my talent to lead great teams effectively. I try hard to respect those people and identify opportunities for their talents to be recognized.

Hope: Expecting More with Unreasonableness

When I started at Walden, I was enjoying my life, even though it was not everything I wanted it to be. I knew that the hard season of life I was in was not all there was for me. I went to work smiling each day with the expectation that something was going to be different soon. No reasonable person would have expected things to change much, but I did. I believed that I would be able to give my daughter a better life. I knew that I was going to be able to use my education for some purpose and some good. I expected more, even when it was not reasonable to do so.

I have been aimless in life. However, becoming a parent helped me gain focus on those things I hoped for in a way that I never had before. I personally want for nothing more than peace of mind, long life, good health, and good relationships, but my hopes for my daughter and this world have no end. I hope for peace, justice, opportunity, space, environmental conservation, and exposure not just for my daughter, but also for the world.

When I became more conscious of what I hoped for as an adult, I was more serious about pursuing it. If you are not longing for something to be different, to go somewhere different, or to inspire people in a different way, you are certainly not likely to get there, and, if you do, you will not recognize it as someplace you wanted to be.

Purpose and Passion: Knowing Yourself

There are many times in life when being authentic is undervalued. If I had tried to be anything other than myself, I would have never been introduced to the opportunity to do my current job. Around 1999, I realized that I wanted to work to focus on the leadership development of marginalized groups of women. I had been working in higher education for a decade and I realized that while I saw a lot of African American women participating in higher education as students, I noticed that they were not taking advantage of the leadership development available to them at the same rate as other groups. I was not really sure that I had what it took to make any real difference in anyone's life, but I knew that I had a passion for the development of African American women. Fifteen years, later, I can tell you that I know that my purpose in life is to act as a conduit for the opportunities and access for African

American women. Although many of my former colleagues saw coming to Walden as a huge risk, I found out shortly after I started working at Walden that I had been given the opportunity to fulfill my purpose because many of the students are women who are marginalized for so many reasons. In my opinion, working at Walden for the last 10 years was divine providence.

The Extraordinary Life: Keeping Your Charge

As aware as I was of the traditional path for success in academia, I knew that path would not work for me. According to conventional professional wisdom, I was supposed to seek out a tenure-track assistant professor position, publish and serve my profession to become tenured, and continue in that same vein until I became a full professor. There is nothing wrong with that life, but that was not going to be my path because I was not going to go all over the country for a job when I needed the support of family and friends as I cared for my daughter. As hard as it can be at times, you have to stay focused on your charge in life and not constantly make comparisons.

People who live ordinary lives constantly compare themselves to other people and never feel satisfied with any moment. But people who live extraordinary lives work hard to make each moment matter. They do not look over their shoulders to see what others behind them or ahead of them are doing. They focus on achieving their personal best as workers, friends, family members, or leaders. They move forward not thinking so much about the end as the process and the discoveries made along the way. They whistle while they work. They pray and meditate in hard situations. They keep getting up and they expect doors to open.

Determination: Honoring Your Journey

I was not afraid when I started my current position. However, I knew that I had to take some chances if I was ever going to live the life my ancestors dreamed of for me. I knew that they had given me a legacy of hard work and determination and if I could be presented with access and opportunity, I could fulfill their hopes for me. I just did not know for a long time that I had anything that resembled the determination of my ancestors, my grandmothers, or my parents. When I discovered that other people saw me as determined, I was a little surprised because I do not compare myself to other people, especially other women in my family. What I know is that any time I feel frustrated or afraid of a new challenge or opportunity, I remind myself that I have opportunities that neither of my grandmothers ever had. They were so much more talented, good, and wise than I can ever hope to be. It is in their names that I move toward, instead of away from, those things that are hard to achieve. I am determined to honor them with good work.

PhD: Holding the Keys

One of the most significant people in any organization is the person who has the keys to the building. While I have learned that having a doctorate does not open every door—some doors are still being held tight to prevent access—a doctorate gives you more keys to unlock doors yourself. You must have the courage to turn your keys to open doors not just to give you access, but to give access to others.

A PhD has not been magic, but I know that it has given me credibility, as well as responsibility. I know that because of my education, family and friends expect me to share with them what I know and to use my education to benefit others. It is not a burden, but it does require me to stay informed and relevant. I have committed myself to a lifetime of education so I can be the best resource for them.

When you are an educator, especially at a university that serves an international audience, you never know when you will cross paths with someone you taught or mentored years before. I am always surprised by the number of former students who tell me that a class I taught was their favorite, how something I said to them changed their direction in life for the better, or how much it matters to them when I rejoice in their accomplishments. I know that the role of an educator is powerful, and I do not take it for granted.

The Transition: Identifying the Right Thing for You

I had tried to move in a variety of directions and there are still things I want to do, but every door does not give you access to your destiny. I have prayed and meditated for a discerning spirit to know which doors should be closed, which doors need a push, and which open doors are actually for me. The most important lesson of my life has been recognizing that I cannot do everything and identifying the right thing for me at the right time.

Reference

Brown, J. (1969). I don't want nobody to give me nothing. On *Sex Machine* [Album]. United States: Polydor Records.

14
Dr. David Bouvin

Professor of Systems Management, Department of Defense

Success in life can be found by leveraging opportunities to assist others with developing purpose, hope, and determination to provide a social good.

The ability to reflect on the importance of purpose, hope, and determination is a foundational component of my personal life. From my early years, I was provided with consistent guidance and unlimited opportunities to continue my educational pursuits. Guidance was provided by parents, schoolteachers, coaches, and civic leaders to focus on the educational process and to reach for the stars. The thought of reaching for the stars is important, because if you fall short of the stars, you can still achieve amazing accomplishments. Continuing your education seems to be one of the more certain approaches to preparing for the future. For example, a person can invest with low returns, purchase real estate within a turbulent housing market, and seek advancement by work alone, but pursuing an education can provide the key to open new doors and opportunities. Another insight I gained from my parents, teachers, coaches, and civic leaders was to not only obtain greatness, but also give back and to assist by encouraging others. Success in life can be found by leveraging opportunities to assist others with developing purpose, hope, and determination to provide a social good.

Purpose and passion are paramount for a happy and productive life. How can a person find happiness without having first developed a purpose and passion for a pursuit, topic, and endeavor? For me, parents, teachers, coaches, and civic leaders assisted with framing a purpose and passion that has never waned. My purpose has been and continues to be empowering others to adopt educational pursuits and to achieve unlimited successes during the process. My journey through the educational process was challenging, life changing, and rewarding. After having completed a doctoral degree and postdoctoral research, the next step was to share the struggle and enormous benefits with others. Sharing reflections, empathy, and recommendations for the educational journey has become a consistent focus in my life to positively influence family, colleagues, acquaintances, and even people I have never met with the endless possibilities for those who adopt educational pursuits.

The topic of hope is a valuable concept to be successful in life. Looking for advancement within the workplace is an arduous process and requires hope. From personal experience, hope can stem from preparation, sustainability, and determination. With regard to preparation, if one prepares for a promotion, then one certainly has a great likelihood of achieving the desired outcome: the promotion. Sustainability is important and serves as an endurance mantra to continue pushing forward even in the face of obstacles. Determination is similar to sustainment and endurance, because one will likely never reach the highest possible goals without a continuous focus of moving forward. Thinking about and implementing hope on a daily basis can be embraced with confidence if one is preparing, sustaining, and maintaining a heightened determination.

The importance of determination should be emphasized within everyone's life. For example, it is likely quite rare to achieve the highest level of accomplishments without a consistent focus and drive. In my personal life, I cannot recall a doctor, lawyer, professor, or military officer who was able to achieve their position in life without having to focus and maintain a heightened determination throughout each step of the process. My life journey has been the same and has had deep roots anchored in determination. I could never have completed an undergraduate degree, served as a military officer in the U.S. Armed Forces, completed a master's degree, earned a doctoral degree, worked as a professor, and completed postdoctoral research without a continued determination throughout each challenge and accomplishment. A consistent focus and determination is necessary during the struggles of one's journey and during times of celebration, because it is always easy to become sidetracked and to lose one's focus.

Reaching one's goals also provides an opportunity to transition from ordinary to extraordinary. From my experience, the lengthy pursuit of earning a doctoral degree is a long process and, at times, becomes ordinary and mundane. However, earning a doctoral degree is life changing and provides for a clear transition from ordinary pursuits to extraordinary experiences and opportunities. For example, a few years after completing my postdoctoral research, I had the opportunity to participate in a consulting engagement within the United Arab Emirates (UAE). Serving as a leader during the consulting project led to meeting established leaders in the Middle East and sharing tea in the palace of a UAE emirate sheikh. Others in attendance for tea included Middle Eastern leaders, a U.S. congressman, lawyers, and fellow doctors. The ability to begin and complete a successful consulting engagement within the UAE is a superb illustration of transitioning from ordinary to extraordinary opportunities in my life.

Completing a doctoral degree has broadened the territory that I am able to serve. I recall my parents, teachers, coaches, and civic leaders encouraging me to continue my educational pursuits; however, it was after completing my doctoral degree that I truly began learning the meaning of accomplishment and how to assist others with reaching their goals. For me, broadening my territory involves a greater ability to serve others by embracing the educational journal and pursuing undergraduate, graduate, and doctoral degrees. For example, for the last 15 years, I have been able to serve as a doctoral mentor, dissertation chair, committee member, and university reviewer for students within the federal government and even those working in a private university environment. In each situation, students can become burdened with the doctoral process; however, positive reinforcement, empathy, and sharing pertinent examples have led to an opportunity to be a positive influence on students from around the world.

To have a positive influence in society, a person must first be able to transform his or her own life positively. For example, during my life, I had the benefit of receiving guidance from visionaries who wanted others to achieve greatness and to reach for the stars. Being able to set off on a path with great expectations was the first step. Continuing the journey with a heightened focus and determination served as the foundation to reach higher and for new accomplishments. Working as a doctoral mentor and dissertation chair provides a continued opportunity to have a positive impact with colleagues from all around the world. Helping others to obtain the goal of a doctoral degree is rewarding and serves as a catalyst for new doctors to have a greater influence on their territory in life, and to encourage others in society continuously to reach for their goals and to embrace educational pursuits.

The ability to reflect on the importance of purpose, hope, and determination is a foundational component of my personal life. From my early years, I was provided with consistent guidance and unlimited opportunities to continue my educational pursuits. Guidance was provided by parents, schoolteachers, coaches, and civic leaders to focus on the educational process and to reach for the stars. The thought of reaching for the stars is important, because if you fall short of the stars, you can still achieve amazing accomplishments. Continuing your education seems to be one of the more certain approaches to preparing for the future. For example, a person can invest with low returns, purchase real estate within a turbulent housing market, and seek advancement by work alone, but pursuing an education can provide the key to open new doors and opportunities. Another insight I gained from my parents, teachers, coaches, and civic leaders was to not only obtain greatness, but also give back and to assist by encouraging others. Success in life can be found by leveraging opportunities to assist others with developing purpose, hope, and determination to provide a social good.

15
Shana Webster-Trotman, PhD, PMP, ITIL

Civil Servant and Educator

Any diamond will tell you that it was just a hunk of coal that stuck to its job and made good under pressure.
—John Mason

The Audacity to Chart a Different Path

Every human being has a purpose to accomplish in life—something that he or she is born or destined to do or to contribute on Earth. For some of us, our purpose has always been clear; from a very young age, we have known what our purpose in life is. Whether our purpose was to be a doctor, lawyer, professor, or philanthropist, we have known it. For others, our purpose has yet to be clearly revealed. Though in both instances, when we walk outside of our purpose, we feel a subtle, yet powerful nudge or tug gnawing at the core of our soul whispering that we are out of alignment with what God placed us on Earth to accomplish. Day in and day out, as we go about our daily routine, we may ask, "Why do others who possess seemingly less aptitude or intellect accomplish exceedingly more? Why are my career aspirations stagnant and yet to manifest? When will I arrive at a point in my life where I know without a doubt that I have found and operate in my purpose?"

Questions such as these stem from an inexplicable feeling of disillusionment that results from functioning or existing in an area where we lack passion. Passion is the zeal that ignites the energy, provides the stamina, and creates the yearning to fulfill our destiny. Passion and purpose share a complimentary relationship. As Warren 2002 noted, "Purpose always produces passion. Nothing energizes like a clear purpose. On the other hand, passion dissipates when you lack purpose." For self-actualization to occur, both must be in agreement, as one cannot thrive without the other.

My purpose in life is to help others accomplish their dream of attaining a college degree. From a very young age, I always had a yearning to teach. At first, I thought that my calling was to teach at the high school level, but as it turns out, my calling is to teach nontraditional adult learners who have—because of life circumstances—delayed working toward their college degree. Being a doctoral degree holder has enabled me to achieve my lifelong goal of being an educator. I have taught as an adjunct professor at the college level since completing my doctoral degree in 2010. Many of my learners have for years, and in some instances even decades, placed the needs of others before themselves. Whether it was caring for young children or ailing parents, lacking the resources to pay for college courses, not having the confidence to believe that they are college worthy, or lacking the stick-to-itiveness to complete the program they started, these are the nontraditional learners that I delight in teaching.

Although society has cast them aside because they have chosen a nontraditional path or do not fit the mainstream American model, these learners often have an uncanny zeal for success. They hunger for it. My work with these learners results in positive social change. After completing her degree, a 45-year-old single mother will not only have the credentials to command a higher salary that enable her to provide for her family, but through the process of pursuing and attaining her degree, she has instilled in her children the importance of education and determination. Her success plants the seed for her children to succeed.

Nontraditional learners are often the first in their family to obtain a college degree, which is a feat I personally relate to. Having grown up on the 32-square-mile island of St. Thomas, U.S. Virgin Islands, and raised by a single mother, I remember always wondering why my classmates seemed to have more than I did regarding their home, attire, cars, and other tangibles. I came to realize that the key to obtaining material assets and social status was education. I grew up not knowing the identity of my father in a household with a mother who struggled to make ends meet. Graduating from high school was a major accomplishment in a community where teenage pregnancy and the high school drop-out rate soared. Unsurprisingly, my mother dropped out of high school when she became pregnant with me and it took 5 years for her to obtain her high school diploma by attending night school. Being fatherless, I was looked down upon by my classmates and adults in the community. Yet it was the pain I witnessed in my mother's eyes as she struggled to keep food on the table, lights on, and clothes on my sister's and my back that resonated with me most. Out of witnessing her despair came hope, my hope for a brighter future and for creating a new paradigm for living. I hoped to be more than a baby-making machine dependent upon the welfare system for shelter and a meal. I hoped to be the first in my family to graduate from college.

Hope is what one desires to see manifest, take place, or transpire despite the countervailing, dismal reality that stares you right in the eyes. Although my childhood was painful, having hope enabled me to see beyond my state of being and past the quagmire of despair surrounding me and dare to envision a future of possibilities where education would enable me to transcend the generational curses of poverty, promiscuity, and illiteracy that plagued my mother, my grandmother, my great-grandmother, and those before them. But to do so, I had to change my thinking and shift my focus from what if's—what if I had a father, what if I came from a family of prominence, what if I were light-skinned—and deal with what is and what could be. Taylor (1995) explains, "The mind is a prolific author. What you believe—along with the action you take—composes your life." I had to have the audacity to believe that a different destiny awaited me, the audacity to believe that I could author my own destiny. I knew that I had no control over where I came from, but I could chart the course ahead.

My third-grade teacher, Mrs. Turnbull, planted the seed of hope. She saw in me something that I did not see in myself. She saw that even though I was dark-skinned with kinky hair, which in the 1970s in the Caribbean was viewed as a negative physical trait, I was smart, beautiful, and outspoken. She helped me to understand that with the grace of God, intelligence and perseverance could take me further in life than physical attributes ever could.

One of my most poignant elementary school memories is of me standing in front of a classroom instructing my fifth-grade peers during one of our daily lunchtime sessions. I was the president, founder, and instructor of the Smurf Club, a voluntary club open to students in the third through fifth grades to help boost reading and comprehension skills. I have always had the desire to teach others and from a very young age, I possessed the ability to bring people together for a common goal, which was a trait Mrs. Turnbull helped cultivate by challenging my thinking. Maxwell (2009) writes, "Gold mines tap out. Stock markets crash. Real estate investments can go sour. But a human mind with the ability to think well is like a diamond mine that never runs out. It's priceless" (p. xi). This is why, when working with nontraditional adult learners, I experience flow, which is "the way people describe their state of mind when consciousness is harmoniously ordered, and they want to pursue whatever they are doing for its own sake" (Csikszentmihalyi, 1990, p. 6). Helping learners develop critical thinking skills is my flow experience.

After having completed a bachelor's degree, two master's degrees, and a doctoral degree, my hope is to create a lasting legacy. I want others to know that they too can accomplish their educational and professional goals and I want to help them do it. According to Maxwell (2009),

> If you are successful, it becomes possible for you to leave an inheritance for others. But if you desire to do more, to create a legacy, then you need to leave that in others. When you think unselfishly and invest in others, you gain the opportunity to create a legacy that will outlive you. (p. 107)

I want to be the Ms. Turnbull in the lives of my learners, the one who speaks positivity into their future.

The road to success is fraught with trials and tribulations. As the adage goes, "nothing worth having ever comes easy." However, with the proper guidance and determination, even the most challenging goals can be accomplished. After all, it is not intelligence that separates those who have earned a doctorate from those who have not; instead, it is perseverance and resilience that separate the haves from the have-nots. Perseverance is the ability to work toward accomplishing a goal, even though life is falling apart around you and others question why you even need a degree or need to earn another degree. Resilience is the ability to get back up and keep trying after experiencing a major life-altering setback, such as the loss of job, failing health, or the passing of a loved one.

In fact, it is from the setbacks and disappointments experienced along my journey that I have gleaned the most. Like a diamond, we too have to go through the fires of life for the potential brilliance that resides in each of us to shine through. My most painful experiences and disappointments have helped to shape my character, humility, and desire to serve others. After graduating from high school, I left St. Thomas and relocated to Alexandria, Virginia with $40 in my possession and an unbridled determination to chart a new path, not just for my personal gratification, but to help others.

Rather than serving others and seeking to effect positive social change, many 21st-century leaders have sought to serve their own agendas and have fallen from prominence because ill-conceived arrogance is their tragic flaw. The notion that the rules do not apply because of one's current position or because of myriad accolades has led to a prevalence of lapses in judgment and a culture in which leadership seeks to exist without integrity and ethics. Thus, regardless of how many rungs I climb on the ladder of success, maintaining a strong sense of self—who I am and what my purpose in life is—and not getting caught up in a false sense of pride remains a priority. Integrity, humility, service, kindness, and a willingness to be the change that they desire to see are the hallmarks of exceptional leaders. These are qualities I seek to emulate.

My journey has not been easy, and I have gleaned many lessons along the way. Purpose, hope, and determination remain present in my life today, and as I continue to set even more challenging goals for myself, I am guided by these nuggets of wisdom.

- Start small and continue to dream big: Regardless of how insurmountable your goal is, start working toward accomplishing it by taking small deliberate steps.
- Be kind to everyone: Treat everyone you meet along your journey with dignity, kindness, and respect. You never know if that person or someone very close to him or her could be your next boss.

- Keep an open mind: Be open to new possibilities, new opportunities, new lessons, and new experiences. Earning a doctorate is not an end to learning; rather, it is one of many destinations on the road to lifelong learning.
- Always seek to serve: Make yourself available to use your talents, skills, and knowledge to help others.
- Beg to differ: You do not always have to agree with those whom you admire. Rather than emulate or imitate others, forge your own identify and seek your own path in life.
- Always give back: Never forget where you came from. Reach back and help others forward.

References

Csikszentmihalyi, M. (1990). *Flow: The psychology of optimal experience.* New York, NY: Harper & Row.

Mason, J. (2008). *You can do it: Even if others say you can't.* Grand Rapids, MI: Spire/Revell.

Maxwell, J. C. (2009). *How successful people think: Change your thinking, change your life.* New York, NY: Center Street.

Taylor, S. L. (1995). *Lessons in living.* New York, NY: Anchor Books.

Warren, R. (2002). *The purpose-driven life: What on earth am I here for?* Grand Rapids, MI: Zondervan.

16
Jodi M. Burchell, PhD

Educator

No one truly knows their purpose in life without personal introspection and examining the resolve of their own existence.

One Joyous Moment at a Time: Finding Purpose and Passion

Examining my purpose is something I did not understand or undertake until I was well into my 40s. I frequently look back on the years before I started my doctoral program and compare them to my life since starting and finishing my doctorate, and I am still amazed by the journey. I did not start my doctoral studies with the intent to discover my purpose or find my passion, but as I look back, that is exactly what happened.

Can purpose and passion be two separate entities? Can you have a true passion for something and not let it have a purpose in your existence? Can you have a true purpose in life without having a passion for that very thing? In my experience, it is not possible to have one without the other. The secret is finding what you are passionate for. Many people wander through life without much of a purpose. If you look closely, those people also lack passion. Your passion does not have to be huge and all encompassing. You do not have to solve world hunger to have passion. I see it every day in parents who devote everything to raising their children. I see it in people who devote themselves to "something." That something could be as simple as rescuing animals or feeding the homeless. That something may mean little to some of us, but may mean everything to an abused animal or to someone who is hungry.

I see passion in educators, much like myself, who give their all to their students. Some may stay up half the night grading papers. That passion is connected to our personal joy. What is joy? There are many definitions, but joy can be described as happiness caused by something particularly satisfying. What is more satisfying than living within and experiencing our own passion? For many of educators, there is a joy in helping students to achieve their dreams of an education. That joy is not realized every day, nor is it usually found in grand gestures. It is usually found in small miracles, like students thanking us for being patient and kind and understanding when some personal issue causes them to falter. Joy may be found in students who comment that you were one of the hardest professors they have had and how much they appreciate that you were. The joy may be in helping students who feel as though they have been abandoned. Joy may be found in helping nontraditional students who are working so hard that you know they are trying to find their own passion and probably, their own purpose. How much joy would it bring you to know that you helped someone discover their own purpose and passion?

Part of the journey is having hope and determination. I can remember being so lost at the beginning of my doctoral journey. All I had to cling to at that moment was hope and the faith that I could persevere and make it through the fog. I had no one to emulate, but I was determined. Eventually, I found my place. I found my mentor, Dr. Walter McCollum, who took me under his wing and gave me a place. He gave me a temporary purpose. He allowed me the opportunity to grow and develop through his peer mentor program. Even then, my true purpose and passion were taking shape. He became a role model for me in so many ways. His life has taken a different path and he has been able to direct his passion and purpose globally. It feeds his soul and I love to see the joy it brings him.

My passion came to be teaching and mentoring students through their doctoral programs. I feel that I have also affected change globally, but in a smaller way through teaching in an online venue. The biggest, most visible contribution is my Vietnamese students. My first exposure to anyone from Vietnam was my now colleague Dr. Kim Tran. Dr. Tran was one of my mentees. We were both in our doctoral journey, but she was behind me in the process. Dr. Tran's first language is not English, so we had a bit of a communication gap, but she had determination the likes of which I had never encountered before. I mentored her as much as I could, and to this day, I know she is grateful for my mentorship. What she does not realize is that I am grateful to her as well. She showed me the true meaning of the word "persevere."

As a professor, I have had the opportunity to teach courses to a satellite school in Hanoi and Ho Chi Minh City, Vietnam. Part of the program involves visiting the students for 2 weeks at the end of their course. I give lectures and finals to the students. I have found that the students are very nervous and eager to do well. For many of them, an education is the only way to help their family rise up out of poverty. Receiving an American MBA means the student holds status in Vietnam. It means that they have worked very hard. Some are only able to work on their studies late at night and get very little sleep for weeks at a time. Some students drive for hours to get to class where tutors help them understand the concepts in English. Many of these students also show me the meaning of the word "persevere." Their drive, their reverence for me as professor, and their gratitude feed my passion and purpose.

It was not my goal to knowingly, purposely transition from ordinary to extraordinary, but I feel like I did, starting with my doctoral journey. People get their doctorates for many reasons. For some, it is just a means to an end. They want to hold a PhD. They want to teach. They want to get a better job. They have something to prove to themselves or to someone. When I started my doctoral journey, I would have stated that I wanted to teach. However, it was more than that. I wanted to transition out of my information technology job and, yes, teach. I was looking for a purpose. I had no passion. As I moved through my doctoral journey, I learned that the possibilities were literally endless. I encountered students who wanted to go back home, to other countries, and open their own schools. I talked to students who worked in every service area and mental health area. I was in awe of their goals. I had my own as well, especially after doing some research about women's access to higher education. I wanted to teach and mentor doctoral students. I wanted to be a role model for women. Yes, you can realize your educational dreams. All it takes is hope, purpose, passion, and determination! I know it is not that easy for some. Some people face many obstacles, including their own personal demons, but obstacles are meant to be overcome.

My world has been enlarged through the many blessings that I have received. I was blessed to have received an angel in my life who mentored me, served as a role model, and showed me the effect one person could have on the world. I was blessed with support from all sides. I was blessed with determination and perseverance. I was blessed with hope and faith. I am not an overly religious person. As a recovering Catholic, I tend to steer clear of organized religion. However, I know all of these blessings came from my higher power. I did not do it alone. He was there with me. I know this to be true.

So, what key principles are most important for your quest to move from ordinary to extraordinary? Start with a lot of personal introspection and determine what your purpose and passion are. Some people's world is not expandable outside of themselves. Their goals may be set and they may not be that extraordinary. Others are constantly seeking to expand their horizons. They want to influence others. They want to affect social change. They see a bigger purpose outside of themselves. They continue to feed their souls through their purpose and passion. They have examined the resolve of their own existence and seek to continue their quest to transition from ordinary to extraordinary every day. They know it is not an end, but rather, a journey. It takes a lot of determination and resolve to get there, but it is worth it. Every time I experience a small miracle, I know it is worth it.

17
Richard T. Brown, Jr., PhD

Associate Campus Dean, IT Consultant

Let determination be the spark you need to bring about social change and hope the fuel you need to see it through.

My Journey from Ordinary to Extraordinary: Purpose and Passion in My Life

Purpose and passion are synonymous in my mind. Both are necessary and both are interchangeable. Although some may find it hard to explain, it is relatively easy for me to describe. I believe my purpose is to help people. It really does not matter in what capacity; as long as I am contributing to another person's well-being, I am fulfilled. As a medic in the U.S. Air Force, I saved lives daily. Now, as a college professor, I am still saving lives. Helping students learn and realize their calling is one of my purposes and provides a level of passion that is very rewarding. I believe we are all put on this Earth for a reason. Some of us are blessed enough to know that reason and embrace it. Some may never know their purpose. I think most people have problems when they try to determine their own purpose. I think we are driven by God, and this almighty force requires us to do what is good in our heart. If we do not, we become self-serving. I think it is nearly impossible to know your true purpose and passion if you are self-serving.

My purpose and passion are driven not by my interests, but by the interests of the people around me. I try to consider the feelings of others with everything that I do. My perspectives have definitely changed since obtaining my PhD. I constantly find myself in positions to help and influence lives around me. People look to me for inspiration and guidance. I try my best to reach all those who need my help. This journey is such a humbling voyage that I feel obligated to give back. As a college professor, I have the unique opportunity to reach eager minds that crave information. So speaking about life experiences or professional triumphs and challenges is part of the daily lessons I provide to my students. I am rewarded when my students come back and thank me for helping to change their life.

Hope in My Life

I think hope is one of the most underrated feelings a person can express. Hope can change your perspective and give you the strength needed to get through trying times. Hope can keep you alive and well. Hope adds meaning to your life. Without it, a person can feel like he or she has no support. I do not think we can live the way that we do without hope. Everything we do is related to hope in some way. We go to work hoping that we can earn money or learn a skill. We take care of our children hoping that they will grow up and be successful and happy. There is no escaping hope.

Without hope, I never would have graduated. I hoped that I could learn what I needed to be successful in the program. I hoped I could learn what I needed to pass my oral presentation. I hoped I could be a PhD who could bring about social change in my community. Hope gives the ability to see the light at the end of the tunnel instead of focusing on every aspect of the journey.

I am most hopeful for God, my family, and my friends. Everything I am and have is a result of one of them. God gives me the purpose and passion to get through life. God also supplies me with all the hope I need to get through any obstacle that comes my way. My family drives my purpose, as it is for them that I strive for perfection at many levels. I hope I am providing them everything they need. As a father, I am constantly thinking about that. Lastly, I am hopeful for my friends as they keep me sane and grounded. I have a small circle of friends who provide me with all the lessons I need. I am most thankful for all the trials and tribulations that I have gone through in life, even though I may not have understood it at the time. Each hurdle has made me stronger and better in many areas.

The Power of Determination

Determination is a powerful tool. Determination gives you the ability to accomplish things you may not have thought you could. Many will argue that determination is built upon a certain set of skills, knowledge, and beliefs, but I believe determination is built upon belief. If you believe you can do something, it will happen. Of course you need to have certain skills to accomplish certain things, but if you understand yourself, you can accomplish anything. Determination is one of the main reasons for my success.

My life has been transformed since graduation. I work in areas and fields that I never thought I would years ago. I have always been a self-driven person, but since obtaining my PhD, I have a new level of self-determination and belief. As a result of making through my program I have been able to take more control of my life. I have been able to work on controlling some of my other skills and take a more active role in mentoring others. I always have family members, friends, students, etc. ask me how I can do some of the things that I do. I tell them it is pure determination. I am determined to maximize my education and use my talents for social change. In my opinion, life is a long journey, so there is no rush to get to certain points in your life. The important point is that you get there and what happens along the way.

My determination has given me the ability to transform minds. I never considered myself a mentor, but I find that I am constantly teaching and providing advice in and out of the classroom. My goal is to help others realize how easy it is to accomplish a task when they are determined to do it. Some are easier to convince than others, so I focus on trying to find that spark in each person to get the determination going. It is an awesome sight when you see it happen. Some people need a stern talk, while others may just need a head nod. Others may need to see you do it first. Each person is different. But I can tell you that determination has changed both my personal and my professional life because I am pretty much the same in both arenas.

Transitioning from Ordinary to Extraordinary

Transitioning from ordinary to extraordinary should happen naturally if you embrace your scholarly identity on your journey. These traits may be different for each person. I think the traits that come out are a result of what you put into your work. One key principle is integrity. You must be true to yourself and those around you at all times. You have to do the right thing, even when no one is looking. People who are not true will eventually expose themselves.

I think courage is another key principle. It can be hard to step out of your comfort zone, but the PhD journey is about challenging yourself. You cannot complete the process if you do not step outside of the box and challenge yourself. If you have a fear of public speaking, think about joining Toastmasters. If you have a problem writing, seek help from a writing center or an editor to overcome that hurdle. If you wish to improve your communication skill, think about attending a workshop on it. These are just some examples of how doing small things can really turn into big things and change your life dramatically.

The third quality is to think of others first. Thinking of others before yourself will help you transform the lives of those around you. I try to do something nice for someone each day. Small acts of kindness can turn into something much larger. It also makes me feel better. I am so much more productive when I feel better.

No Ordinary Life Here

As a doctoral degree holder, my territory has expanded exponentially. I work, teach, and consult in corporate America and in academia. I find myself partnering with other professionals on a variety of topics ranging from organizational culture to emotional intelligence to curriculum design. I am also being offered opportunities that I never applied for or showed an interest in before I completed my degree. The majority of the opportunities come from networking and talking to different people as I come across them daily.

Having a PhD has totally changed my perspective and helped me achieve extraordinary things. There is no limit to what I can do, or at least I think there isn't. I learned early in the doctoral process from my mentor and dissertation chair that extraordinary things should be expected. Dr. McCollum leads by example, and you have no choice but to see the value in his approach. This same approach has helped me achieved my goals, both personally and professionally. I thank him each time I see him.

Key Lessons Learned and Words of Wisdom

One of the main lessons learned is to be an active listener and keep an open mind. Being an active listener includes things like not cutting a person off as they are speaking. When you do that, you are not truly listening to the person, as you are subconsciously preparing your rebuttal. Active listening also includes restating what you just heard the speaker say as confirmation. Asking clarifying questions is a form of active listening that shows the speaker that you are engaged in what was said.

Keeping an open mind is another important trait. When you have an open mind, you are open to suggestions, perspectives, possibilities, and opportunities. This is critical when having discussions or interactions with others. You need to be able to embrace different views, interests, and suggestions. If you can master these two tips, you may find yourself more engaged in conversations and possible leading some new initiative. Cheers!

18
Saul Santiago, PhD

District Director, Data and Assessments
U.S. Virgin Islands Department of Education

What I've learned most about myself through my academic journey is just how much untapped potential I had to create a positive social impact in my community, by applying hope, purpose, and determination to my personal and professional goals.

Hope in the Virgin Islands: Using Research to Improve Student Outcomes

My academic journey helped define my professional purpose and focus my passion for positive social change in my community. My work for U.S. Virgin Islands Department of Education, a low-income, high-poverty school district, received new meaning as I started to understand the power of purpose, hope, and determination. I made a decision for my own children to attend public schools, which added a more personal sense of urgency to my efforts to improve student outcomes for every student in the U.S. Virgin Islands. Districts in low-income areas often depend on community involvement to fill in the asset gap, including help from local businesses that volunteer time and resources.

The focus of my doctoral research was understanding small business owners' attitudes toward their community and the effect, if any, their attitude had on their level on engagement in the community. My interactions with small business owners and the data from my doctoral research indicated a strong engagement level. This finding, combined with my research on the power of public–private partnerships, solidified my determination to improve public education through data, research, and community engagement. By purposefully approaching my work, including the data that I interpret and the educators I interact with, I can do my part to steer the direction of public education in my community. Viewing my tasks through the lens of creating lasting, positive change in my community allows me to be more confident in my research on current student outcomes, more determined in changing organizational culture toward individual and collective responsibility, and more purposeful in my prescriptions for change.

I grew increasingly hopeful for the future of the U.S. Virgin Islands as my academic journey unfolded. Through my work for the local Department of Education, I visit schools, classrooms, and computer labs full of students. I see their optimism and their willingness to engage in learning, even in the midst of aging school facilities. I see them striving, even as teachers and administrators deal with technology challenges that, were they fully functional, would offer many more tools for education. I see the results of standardized testing as a wake-up call to the educators, administrators, and indeed the entire community, signaling that we must work harder to ensure we provide our children with the necessary tools to succeed. My hope is that we can meet that challenge and allow each public school student in the U.S. Virgin Islands to reach his or her full potential. My academic journey allows me to view my professional journey in a new light and to seek out the grand, perhaps idealistic, goals that otherwise would seem out of reach. These goals include identifying research-driven solutions that help educators, administrators, and other staff at the Department of Education to improve student outcomes effectively, despite the socioeconomic challenges inherent in a high-poverty school district.

Orienting toward more ambitious professional and personal goals requires renewed and strengthened determination to overcome existing and unforeseen obstacles. In my professional life, determination allows for overcoming limitations in resources and support. Without a dedicated vehicle to drive to schools for professional development, the easy solution is to scale back engagements and plan for virtual professional development seminars. Yet our student data indicates a strong need to have on-site and hands-on professional development for educators, so I'm determined to be at every opportunity offered to me, even if I have to use my own vehicle to get there. Determination helps to guide me past colleagues who are reluctant to adapt to the requirements of a shifting curriculum, to the demands of preparing students using college and career-ready standards, and to the expectations of the new job market that awaits students.

Part of the transition in moving to more expansive goals of impacting social change from more ordinary career and personal goals involved depending on key principles to guide me. The principles included accountability, the conviction that I stand by my work, and the results of it. Another of my guiding principles is transparency, which involves ensuring I share my data, my tools, my processes, and my insight with all appropriate stakeholders. Transparency includes being honest regarding tools, software, curriculum, and approaches that bear no fruit in student outcome data. Finally, one of my key guiding principles is respect, which means assuming the best in persons I interact with and taking the standard position that they are all professionals with the best intentions and a common goal of improving education. It also means separating personal relationships from professional relationships, as well as truly listening to and internalizing the input from every member of the educational community.

As a newly minted doctoral degree holder, my work within the U.S. Virgin Islands Department of Education continues to center on using data to improve the education of our public school students and thus the future direction of these islands. As one of many administrators in the department, my role is both narrow and wide ranging. It is narrow in the way I focus on the issue of student performance on assessments, and it is wide ranging in my search for factors that directly and indirectly impact how students learn. These factors include obvious educational factors such as instructional time, teacher quality, and curriculum. Yet societal factors such as parental involvement, family income levels, housing, and culture are just as important. Using my doctoral research skills in my capacity as district data director is one way to effect potentially extraordinary change in the U.S. Virgin Islands.

The doctoral journey provided key lessons and personal anecdotes that have influenced my thinking and refined how I view myself and my ability to impact social change in the U.S. Virgin Islands. What started as an inward goal of furthering my education and career prospects eventually morphed into an outward goal as I learned from my mentor and peers how they used the tools of academic research to create real, meaningful change in the world. From my mentor's focus on humanitarian efforts in Haiti to the research emphasis of my peers, which included efforts to reduce recidivism, my internal compass shifted toward creating outward value with the skills I was developing.

I've grown both personally and professionally. Personally, my family has grown and given me an even sharper perspective on the important work I do for public education and on ensuring my children and every other child receives a quality education, which is a critical component in uplifting our community. Professionally, my growth from systems analyst to human resources assistant director and eventually to district director mirrored my intellectual growth as I advanced through my doctoral studies. Academically, a new understanding of research, data, and academic rigor provides a solid foundation to identify solutions to the seemingly intractable educational problems faced by my local community. What I've learned most about myself through my academic journey is just how much untapped potential I had to create a positive social impact in my community, by applying hope, purpose, and determination to my personal and professional missions.

Prior to my dissertation, I conducted research modules that dealt with leadership and public education. Along with my dissertation, I now have a solid foundational base of completed research that I'm proud of, and I'm excited about making my work more public and having it make a positive social impact. In terms of future research, my passion is for public education and improving it, and I want to use the skills I developed working on my dissertation to carry out more research in that area, specifically on student testing, teacher quality, and any connections between them. Having completed my academic journey, I'm not in the midst of a personal and professional journey to create lasting, positive change in the U.S. Virgin Islands public school system. Instead, I'm excited about taking advantage of the knowledge, skills, and methods I developed working alongside my mentor and colleagues and using them for the benefit of the local public school system and beyond.

19
Terrance Campbell, MA Ed, MSISM

Deputy Director – YOUR Center

Trust in the Lord with all thine heart; and lean not unto thine own understanding. In all thy ways acknowledge him, and he shall direct thy paths.

For me, one's purpose is that which one is driven to do, whether in one's native hometown, away at school, or in a new community. I was raised to believe that our primary goal in life is to identify what God's purpose for you is and to make that the tool by which the world sees Him through you. For me, determination is a person's resolve in identifying and pursuing his or her purpose, in spite of the trials and tribulations that pursuit is fraught with. For me, faith is the evidence of things hoped for, the evidence of things not seen (Hebrews 11:1). So, for me, when you are following the purpose that God has for you with determination the size of a mustard seed, you truly can move mountains and obtain anything that you hope for

(Matthew 17:20). Or as I like to tell youth that I come in contact with, "Step into your greatness."

Ensuring the health and wellness of the American citizenry has historically been one of the many purposes of my family, from my grandfather serving as a staff sergeant during World War II in Italy, to my grandmother serving as a nurse for over 30 years, to my father serving in Vietnam, to my mother serving as a HIV/AIDS prevention and awareness practitioner scholar for over 30 years. In 1983, I took my first steps toward my purpose of being an informatics and information systems security practitioner scholar, in the seventh grade with a third-generation 8-bit computer with a 6502 CPU running at 1.79 MHz commonly known as an Atari 800 XL. However, unlike my friends and neighbors, I received a stack of electronic gaming magazines rather than a stack of video games. I took this as an opportunity to challenge the CEO in me to develop my knowledge, skills, and abilities (KSAs) in computer science programming to enhance my company's (paper route) profitability. Within a couple of months, I had developed a crude version of QuickBooks in BASIC. Within the first 6 months after using the new program, I received two pay increases and my customer-base increased by roughly 11%.

My computer science KSAs increasing sparked interest in other sciences, including martial science/martial arts. This led to me investing some of the revenue in myself in the form of formal martial arts lessons across a host of disciplines. These three activities (computer science, a paper route, and martial arts) provided me with a daily of dose of career and technical education that required a high degree of project planning and implementation. From the seventh to the 11th grades, I focused on developing my own unique way of using computer science principles to design systems for solving problems more effectively, which today is a field of research and practice known as computation thinking (Lempinen & Rajala, 2014). I began to see a direct relationship between my computer science prowess and academic performance; including earning mostly A's and B's in Physics, Chemistry I and II, Biology I and II, Algebra I and II, Geometry, and Trigonometry. Further, the routine immersion of theories, theorems, and proofs led me in the 10th grade to a theory to help me better understand how technology (including computer science) could be used to enhance business efficiency and productivity: the sociotechnical systems theory (Figure 1), which focuses on how the interrelatedness of social and technical aspects of an organization or society impact productivity and efficiency, also known as joint optimization (Griffith, Campbell, Allen, Robinson, & Kretman, 2010; Kull, Ellis, & Narasimhan, 2013). Since then, I have made a strong distinction between technology and office automation, with technology referring to processes or methodologies used to collect, process, and disseminate information (Evangelou & Karacapilidis, 2005; Griffith, Campbell, et al., 2010) and the focus of office automation being integrating digital hardware, software, or infrastructure to enhance the efficiency, productivity, scope, or reach of technology (Evangelou & Karacapilidis, 2005; Griffith, Campbell, et al., 2010; Kull et al., 2013).

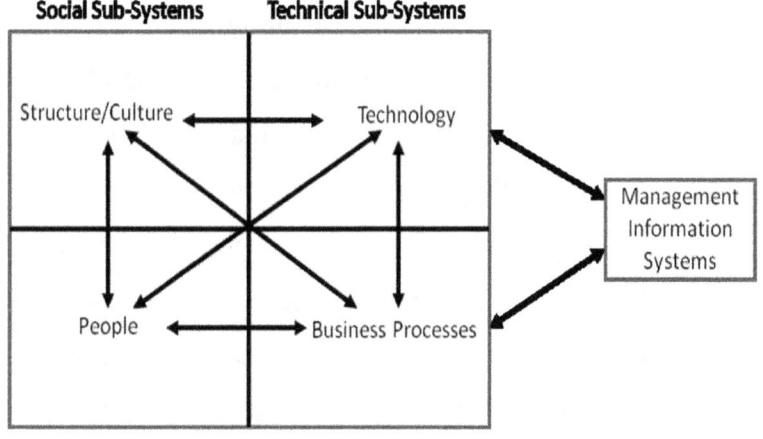

Figure 1: Sociotechnical systems

During the spring of my junior year in high school, my counselor brought to my attention a summer college immersion program called AIM (Academically Interested Minds) at the General Motors Institute (now Kettering University). Founded in 1984 in Flint, Michigan, AIM is a highly competitive, free, residential, precollege summer program for high school juniors. Participants from across the United States, Canada, Mexico, Puerto Rico, and the Caribbean attend college freshman-level courses in calculus, chemistry, computer programming, economics, physics, and business management taught by Kettering University faculty. Monday through Thursday, participants attend classes with homework assignments, quizzes, and exams. On Fridays, participants go on company tours and interact with engineers and managers. Candidates must have had 2 years of high school English, 2 years of high school algebra or the equivalent preparation, 1 year of geometry, and 1 year of high school chemistry with lab with a minimum grade point average of 3.0 in each class. Because I was accepted into the AIM program, I made the hard decision to sell my business. But as a result of my performance, I earned a high-school co-op job with my sponsor AC Rochester (now Delphi) during my senior year and worked as a database administrator in the Accounting

Department for one of my assignments. This experience resulted in me earning a 3-year Civil Engineering Co-op with the State of Michigan.

In addition to working for Delphi during my senior year in high school, I also competed in the Annual Wolverine Baptist District Oratorical Contest in 1989 and won using the theme "faith and technology as a tool for reducing teen pregnancy and other chronic illnesses." However, in the summer of 1989, my biological grandmother lost her fight with ovarian cancer. Her last words to me were, "Use your computer skills to help make the world a better place for all." I was devastated; however, I took her request as God revealing my purpose, for I firmly believed He hadn't brought me that far to leave me alone. Since that time, I have been determined to become an accomplished informatics and information systems security practitioner scholar. Fast forward 25 years, and I am a seasoned 30+ year operations-management-focused information technology (IT) professional with a strong research background that possess two master's degrees (information systems management and education) and several industry-recognized certifications (IT and public health). During this time, I assisted in founding a faith-based HIV prevention agency known as YOUR Center (YC). In 1999, YC developed and implemented H.O.P.E. parties (HIV Outreach, Prevention, and Education) throughout Flint and Genesee County. These parties use naturally occurring social networks to help individuals and groups identify individual, community, and policy-level factors that increase their HIV risk (Griffith, Pichon, Campbell, & Allen, 2010; Hadid & Afshin Mansouri, 2014).

In 2004, YC collaborated with the National Coalition of Pastors' Spouses (NCPS) to expand the H.O.P.E. curriculum into a manual for the faith community that is endorsed by the U.S. Department of Health and Human Services (Contract #03T480223). This project helped YC leaders to develop a deeper understanding of one of the most overlooked facts about faith-based organizations: they have an organizational structure that in some cases is regional and national in scope (Figure 2). Aligned with social capital research, YC witnessed the impact of trust on faith leaders' capacity to engage their congregation in the fight against HIV (Griffith, Pichon, et al., 2010; Hadid & Afshin Mansouri, 2014).

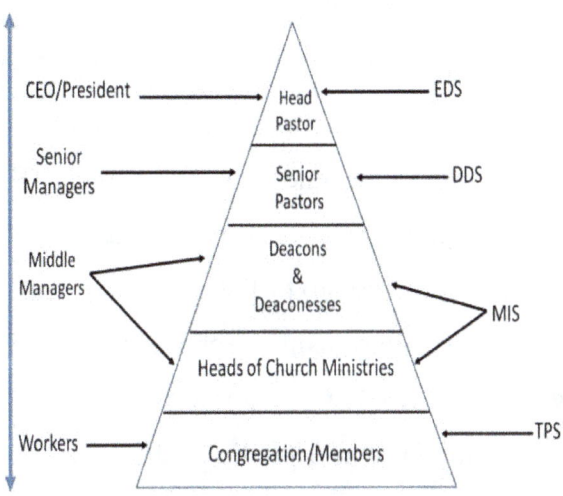

Figure 2: Sociotechnical systems theory diagram

Historically, trust has been viewed as a psychological condition comprised of two dimensions: cognitive and affective. The cognitive dimension focuses on impacting end-users' willingness to have faith in a vendor's competence and reliability. The affective dimension focuses on impacting the confidence end-users place in a product or service provider based on the provider's level of connectedness. Combining the two results in technology and/or OA (T&OA) trust, which is the willingness of leadership to adopt and use T&OA to develop new behaviors. Looking at FBOs as organizations, YC began to see that process as HIV prevention and awareness capacity-building technology for faith-leaders, their spouses, and their congregations, both individually and collectively, with capacity defined as the application of KSAs to faith leaders' roles and confidence in using those KSAs to strategically integrate HIV-prevention best practices to their ministries. In the context of sociotechnical theory, for YC, this translated into using technology to help FBO leaders develop the KSAs needed to establish and sustain a culture for viewing HIV as a public health issue rather than a moral issue within the context of their doctrine and then to identify customized business processes to engage in the fight against HIV. This aligns with a relative new field of practice and research called consumer health informatics.

Consumer health informatics (CHI) seeks to investigate the impact of integrating consumers' needs and preferences into the design and use of OA on their health-care-related activities, including health literacy. Health literacy is an individual's or group's capacity to obtain, understand, and communicate health information systems and services to make positive health decisions (American Medical Association, 2010; Marshall, Henwood, & Guy, 2012). The significance of this is that poor health literacy is a stronger predictor of health status than age, income, education level, employment status, and race. Moreover, culture directly affects health literacy, and the utility of health literacy is directly impacted by a person's level of comfort and amount of use, as with most any tool. For YC, it was clear that FBOs could be mobilized against HIV more broadly; however, YC lacked a statistically significant approach for accomplishing this objective. So, YC's executive team (including me) focused on transforming the faith community manual it developed with NCPS into a CHI-informed evidence-based framework for mobilizing FBOs against HIV. From 2000 to 2010, the Centers for Disease Control and Prevention and the Association of Schools of Public Health comanaged a program for HIV prevention program managers in minority-based, community-based organizations known as the Institute for HIV Prevention Leadership (IHPL; Painter, Ngalame, Lucas, Lauby, & Herbst, 2010; Richter et al., 2006). Using the socioecological model of public health and strategic management principles, IHPL fellows built the capacity to apply new KSAs to develop new evidence-based interventions or enhance existing HIV prevention and awareness interventions. Upon the completion of IHPL, each fellow had developed a full proposal that he or she could market to obtain funding.

In 2005, using Eexecutive Director Bettina Campbell's IHPL project as the foundation, YC convened a community advisory board of local pastors and their spouses, together with Derek Griffith, PhD and the late Kevin Robinson, PhD to transform the NCPS's manual into a capacity-building technology for mobilizing faith leaders against HIV. At the same time, I was completing my PhD coursework in learning and knowledge management at Walden University, where I met Dr. McCollum, who agreed to supervise the successful completion of my knowledge area modules. Although, I had successfully completed my coursework and the modules, the dearth of CHI-informed research for FBOs made identifying a dissertation-worthy project a challenge that I couldn't overcome. However, I continued to forge forward with YC's executive team developing a capacity-building technology for mobilizing faith leaders and FBOs against HIV called YOUR Blessed Health that was funded by the Ruth Mott Foundation from 2006 to 2013. Some of YOUR Blessed Health's highlights to date include YC (a) raising the awareness of the social, economic, and national security impact of HIV in over 50,000 Genesee County residents in 80 FBOs across nine denominations; (b) producing over 20 published articles; (c) assisting in the creation and implementation of a mandatory HIV-awareness-focused service-learning class for University of Michigan—Flint campus incoming freshman in 2010; (d) serving as the co-principal investigator for University of Michigan's School of Public Health 2009–2014 social media and HIV core research project; and (e) serving as the lead HIV prevention and informatics agency for the National Faith Mobilization Network.

In 2006, in an attempt to expand the reach and scope of YOUR Blessed Health by leveraging the influence of the sport and entertainment industry, YC collaborated with an outreach program for Wayne State University College of Education Department of Kinesiology, Health Science and Sport Studies called the Volunteer, Administrators and Coaches Program (WSU/COE/VAC) to create, implement, and evaluate a Sport and Technology Academy. The focus of the Sport and Technology Academy continues to be on using T&OA to engage and expose youth to nontraditional sports, nontraditional bench players, and the role CHI plays in the entertainment industry as a whole. In 2010, I participated in IHPL and focused my project on developing a research- and project-based experience on using digital media to create and disseminate to enhance the health literacy of individuals focused on HIV prevention and awareness known the $S^2TE^2A^2M^3$ Career Club. Some of The $S^2TE^2A^2M^3$ Career Club's highlights to date include (a) four published articles with three in press and a special edition for *Frontiers in Public Health* being developed; (b) assisting over 750 individuals obtain employment with organizations such as Ford, Apple, Comcast, and Hewlett Packard; (c) assisting Chinese Ministry of Education consultants design a strategy for using SCRATCH as China's next-generation K-12 workforce mobilization strategy, (d) me being asked to oversee the finals for the first video game development competition in the Michigan Science Olympiad, and (e) me serving as the project director for one of the first cybersecurity training programs in the United States that employs simulations and digital game-based learning.

YOUR Center's body of work continues to provide me with daily life lessons. Three have become guiding principles for my daily walk with GOD:

1. Knowing your purpose is one thing, but having the tenacity to endure your "walk through the valley of the shadow of death" is quite another. As Kate Williams says, "Haters are going to hate." But in

His name you rebuke them, praise Him, and make it do what it does.

2. If my people, who are called by my name, shall humble themselves, and pray, and seek my face, and turn from their wicked ways, then will I hear from heaven, and will forgive their sin, and will heal their land (2 Chron. 7:14). All of the highlights in this chapter speak to this happening directly.

3. Throughout history, visionaries have not been welcomed readily. However, don't let people block your blessing; even those that call you their friend or have been your mentor for a season.

In closing, we often forget that in the Garden of Gethsemane, Jesus Christ acknowledged that He didn't want to die; however, said let the purpose You have for me be fulfilled. So, what purpose has He revealed to you and what are you doing to bring it to fruition? Carpe Diem!

References

American Medical Association. (2010). Health literacy and patient safety: Help patients understand. Retrieved from http://www.ama-assn.org/ama1/pub/upload/mm/367/healthlitclinicians.pdf

Badinelli, R., Barile, S., Ng, I., Polese, F., Saviano, M., & Nauta, P. D. (2012). Viable service systems and decision making in service management. *Journal of Service Management, 23*, 498-526.

Evangelou, C., & Karacapilidis, N. (2005). On the interaction between humans and knowledge management systems: A framework of knowledge sharing catalysts. *Knowledge Management Research & Practice, 3*(4), 253-261.

Griffith, D. M., Campbell, B., Allen, J. O., Robinson, K. J., & Kretman, S. (2010). YOUR Blessed Health: An HIV prevention program bridging public health and faith communities. *Public Health Reports, 125*(Suppl 1), 4-11.

Griffith, D. M., Pichon, L., Campbell, B., & Allen, J. O. (2010). YOUR Blessed Health: A faith-based, CBPR approach to addressing HIV/AIDS among African Americans. *AIDS Education and Prevention, 22*, 203-217.

Hadid, W., & Afshin Mansouri, S. (2014). The lean-performance relationship in services: A theoretical model. *International Journal of Operations & Production Management, 34*(6), 750.

Kull, T. J., Ellis, S. C., & Narasimhan, R. (2013). Reducing behavioral constraints to suppliers' integration: A socio-technical systems perspective. *Journal of Supply Chain Management, 49*, 64-86.

Lempinen, H., & Rajala, R. (2014). Exploring multi-actor value creation in IT service processes. *Journal of Information Technology, 29*, 170-185.

Marshall, A., Henwood, F., & Guy, E. S. (2012). Information and health literacy in the balance: Findings from a study exploring the use of ICTs in weight management. *Library Trends, 60*, 479-496.

Painter, T. M., Ngalame, P. M., Lucas, B., Lauby, J. L., & Herbst, J. H. (2010). Strategies used by community-based organizations to evaluate their locally developed HIV prevention interventions: Lessons learned from the CDC's innovative interventions project. *AIDS Education and Prevention, 22*, 387-401.

Richter, D. L., Potts, L. H., Prince, M. S., Dauner, K. N., Reininger, B. M., Thompson-Robinson, M., . . . Jones, R. (2006). Development of a curriculum to enhance community-based organizations' capacity for effective HIV prevention programming and management. *AIDS Education and Prevention, 18*, 362-374.

20
Walter R. McCollum, PhD

Educator/President, McCollum Enterprises, LLC
Executive Director, Walter McCollum Education Foundation

Every great dream begins with a dreamer. Always remember, you have within you the strength, the patience, and the passion to reach for the stars to change the world.
—Harriet Tubman

Dreaming is something that I've always done! I remember growing up in a small town in South Carolina, dreaming of a better life, dreaming of opportunities to travel the world and earn an education, and dreaming of using my life to change the world in some way. Dreams were all that I had to hold onto in the midst of the plights and social conditions that surrounded me. I grew up as an only child in the 60s and 70s in a single-parent household where my mother worked two jobs to provide for me. My father did what he could to provide for me, but with another family of his own, he was stretched thin. I had a village of family members who stood in the gap for both my mother and father because of the love they had for us as family. My parents only lived 9 miles apart, so it was relatively easy for both sides of the family to come together to provide love and support. Both sides of the family are like one big family. In fact, my mother and father have always been friends and still are to this day. I can literally say, "It takes a village to raise a child."

I'm fortunate and very grateful that I was reared by and had the opportunity to know both sets of great-grandparents. There are so many wonderful experiences and lessons learned that contribute to the extraordinary man I've become. My maternal great-grandparents owned a farm that included almost every farm animal imaginable. I would follow Grandpa to milk the cows, plow the fields, cut pulpwood, bail hay, feed the chickens and hogs, and so much more. I would watch Grandma churn butter and buttermilk, gather eggs from the nests, and pick every fruit and vegetable there was to eat—peas, beans, potatoes, tomatoes, corn, okra, peanuts, strawberries, and blackberries. Boy, those homemade blackberry and strawberry pies were delicious! The work ethic was strong on both sides of the family. I am thankful to my late great-grandparents for instilling a good work ethic in me at a very young age. My paternal great-grandparents and grandparents were my rock and foundation. They kept me in church and grounded in the word of God. They were very empathetic and supportive, understood the plights and social conditions that I faced, and always encouraged me to continue fighting and pushing through. My grandfather, stood in the gap for my father and would talk with me about life, education, and changing the world. I remember Papa retiring from Draper Corporation after working there for over 40 years, serving the elderly in his community, serving as an honorary deacon in his church, serving as Santa for the children in the community, and giving his last dime to help someone. He was a family man, modest and humble, with a quiet spirit. I would always dream of being like him. Little did I know that my dream would come true and I would continue his legacy.

When I was 7 years old, I awoke from a dream in which I was walking across a stage in a cap and gown to receive a diploma. I heard the name "Dr. Walter McCollum," but the visual was a reflection of a child walking across the stage to receive his diploma. Unbeknownst to me, God was showing me a glimpse of the beginning of a profound life leading to positive social change. I shared the dream with

Papa, and he encouraged me to earn the highest level of education possible and be an example for others in the community to follow. That is what I did. After graduating from high school, I entered the U.S. Air Force at the age of 17. I wasn't old enough to enlist, so my father signed for me to enlist. That was the best decision I could have made to change the trajectory of my life from growing up in a small town where there were high rates of domestic abuse, drug and alcohol abuse, broken families, and sexual abuse. I have lost relatives to cirrhosis of the liver due to drinking alcohol every day. I lived through the trauma of seeing my mother and other women beaten by men. These experiences, compounded with friends of the family attempting to molest me, led to a state of manic depression and to suicide attempts. This was during an era when many parents provided for their children but were not equipped to nurture, guide, and provide practical support to them. Pathological behavior is passed down from generation to generation. Until someone decides to break the cycle and break the curse, the behavior is passed on continuously. I broke the cycle and broke the curse. It wasn't until I broke the pathological behavior that I was able to connect with my purpose and passion. Our lives are often consumed with so much stuff, baggage, and brokenness that we are not able to see the forest for the trees. We are often so busy that we don't have the quietness or solitude needed to align to our faith, which is a key ingredient to aligning with purpose and passion.

I've often heard that purpose and passion are birthed from pain. I believe this is true, as the years of pain that I lived through definitely led me to my purpose. During my years in the Air Force, I enrolled in college, joined various ministries in church, and volunteered in communities where I was stationed. Despite the aftermath from the plights I had experienced, I was still holding onto my dreams and trying to apply the foundational principles that I learned growing up. Concurrently, I went through years of counseling to overcome the trauma and depression I was experiencing. I'm grateful that I didn't fall prey to the idea that going to counseling is a sign of weakness and a stigma. Little did I know that I would write a book for men titled *Strength of a Black Man: Destined for Self-Empowerment* to encourage Black men to go to counseling to overcome thoughts of suicide or other plights they faced, such as absentee fathers, lack of supportive and positive role models and mentors, physical abuse, domestic abuse, and even sexual abuse.

I traveled the world while serving in the Air Force. Over my 13-year service obligation, I was stationed at Langley Air Force Base, Hampton, Virginia; Clark Air Base, Philippines; Ellsworth Air Force Base, Rapid City, South Dakota; Incirlik Air Base, Turkey; Virginia Military Institute, Lexington, Virginia; and Bolling Air Force Base and the Pentagon, Washington DC. In the Philippines, I started to connect with my purpose and passion of serving in international countries. I was only 19 and felt a need to engage in the betterment of humankind. Right outside the military base, small children would be living in cardboard boxes. Some had no clothes and looked like they hadn't eaten in months. Through the base chapel, I would help men in the men's ministry volunteer to set up food camps and clothing drives. It was the most rewarding feeling to be able to help someone who was less fortunate and to contribute to eradicating child homelessness. I would reflect back on the conversations I had with my grandfather when he said, "When you help someone who is less fortunate than you are, change will occur."

It wasn't until I served in Turkey that I became very serious about my purpose and passion in life. I knew that my ministry was in missions and serving the greater good because I felt an indescribable feeling every time I would provide service in underserved communities. I learned this attribute from my grandfather. He was a great servant and impacted so many lives through his spirit of generosity and giving. I served in various ministries at the base chapel, including Usher Board, Young Adult Choir, and Men's Ministry. Upon my return to the states, I continued to serve in Men's Ministry and Military Ministry at various churches, which provided me the opportunity to get involved in various initiatives, including mentoring young men, supporting the homeless, supporting veterans, and empowering youth. My last job in the military was under the Clinton administration in the Office of the Secretary of Defense, Public Affairs. Yes, Monica Lewinsky and I worked in the same office and knew each other! In this position, I began to place a great emphasis on mentoring young men of color. Many young men of color don't make it out of South Carolina, and the chances of making it to the Office of the Secretary of Defense in the Pentagon are slim to none. During that time, I was working on my master's degree and encouraged young men to earn the highest level of education possible to become empowered in all areas of their lives. I was very capable of providing young men with this insight, as I had begun a path of healing to become self-empowered in many areas of my own life. I started mentoring young men in Washington, DC, public schools both personally and professionally. It was also during this time when I knew that my life had a greater purpose to impact change on a much larger scale than in the local communities I was serving.

Sometimes when your life flashes before your eyes, you begin to reflect on how much greater you can be. I had this reflection on 9/11 when the plane hit the Pentagon. I had discharged from the military a few years prior and had begun my corporate career. I was working for Lockheed Martin in the Pentagon when the plane hit the building. I knew several of the people who were killed in the tragic event and to this day I continue to go to the Pentagon on 9/11 each year to commemorate with the families of the victims to celebrate the lives of their loved ones. As I look back over my life, I am thankful and declare the best gift that I have ever received was the gift of life. My birthday is September 12th, and God spared me to see the very next day after 9/11, another birthday. I'm grateful for life, as I was later shown that my life is an example of how a person's past doesn't determine the future and how a person can transition from ordinary to extraordinary by creating a legacy and body of work to change the world.

Throughout my 14-year corporate career, I continued to stay connected to service in some way. My last job in the corporate world was with Sodexo. I was the senior director of organizational change for North America. In that role, I was also the national chairperson for HONOR, a military business resource group, which consisted of over 500 military veterans and spouses. The focus of our strategy was to support and serve active, guard, and reserve military members and their spouses in the community. This was a rewarding way to serve the community because I had served 13 years in the Air Force and knew the challenges that military members had with transitioning from military to the corporate world and the lack of support they were provided after serving and protecting our country. I was able to partner with military organizations such as Paralyzed Veterans of America and Disabled American Veterans. During that time, I also served on the board of directors for Community for Creative Non-Violence in Washington, DC, which is the largest homeless shelter in the United States. While on the board, I worked with the homeless population, many of whom were veterans, on career development skills, life skills, and any support they needed to transition back into mainstream society.

During the process of earning my PhD and transitioning from the corporate world to higher education, my purpose and passion was confirmed and validated. I attended Walden University to earn my doctoral degree after speaking with a colonel I worked with in the Air Force who was working on completing his PhD there. He told me that he thought I should consider Walden because of my previous life's work in social change. This was a perfect fit because the center of Walden's mission is social change. As I went through my doctoral process, I connected more with my purpose and passion and began to use them both to impact positive change in the world on a global scale. While in the program, I began a student cohort of doctoral students in the nation's capital and peer-mentored them in the areas of research methods and provided them with resources and support to help them meet their educational goals and objectives. By creating this peer-mentoring model, I would later have job opportunities in higher education and a platform to mentor my own doctoral learners and increase graduation and retention rates at several universities. As a result, I've not only been able to encourage and empower young men of color to continue their education, but I've graduated men of color with PhDs—the highest level of education! This is impacting positive social change through purpose and passion by serving and mentoring! The peer-mentoring model has since been adopted by other universities, and results are showing students have a greater chance of completing doctoral programs when they are in peer-mentoring and cohort models. In my 10 years in higher education, I have chaired dissertation committees and graduated over 50 doctoral students! I call them "McCollum Scholars!"

I have made a lifelong commitment to impacting positive social change in countries such as Costa Rica, South Africa, and Haiti. In Cahuita, Costa Rica, I led a delegation and assessed international development opportunities on an indigenous reservation and rebuilt homes to coincide with the Costa Rican culture of cooking on open fire. I also conducted workshops on leadership development and Emotional Intelligence to help locals have a greater understanding of concepts around mutual respect and self-dignity. In Komga, Eastern Cape, South Africa, I collaborated with an AIDS orphanage and local hospital to establish partnerships with U.S. organizations. I also mentored an educator in a local township on the teacher certification process and establishing a nonprofit organization.

After the devastation of the earthquake in Port au Prince, Haiti, I made a personal connection to the Haitian culture and their plight. The first time I went to Haiti was with a Christian organization on a missions trip. I have since travelled to Haiti several times a year for the past 5 years. I've had the opportunity to do some great work in Haiti, which include establishing a mentoring program for young men between the ages of 16 and 22 and coaching the young men on principles of servant leadership. I've also led delegations in Haiti to rebuild areas destroyed by natural disasters and explore opportunities to bring technology into the Haitian education system. I've had the opportunity to meet with the minister of education's cabinet on opportunities to pilot technology platforms in the school system. My ultimate goal is to build a school in Haiti for young men with a focus on science, technology, engineering, and math.

People often ask me why I don't invest in education in the United States rather than going to Haiti. When you are clear on your purpose and passion, no one can deter you or discourage you to do otherwise. I'm very clear that my eternal purpose and passion is to contribute to international development through mentoring and service. That clarity came through connecting with my faith early in my life, applying the foundational principles of service, and mentoring and becoming emotionally and culturally intelligent. Emotional Intelligence is paramount on the path to seeking clarity on purpose and passion. When you are self-aware about navigating your emotional landscape, you become more in tune with what motivates you intrinsically, you become more empathetic about using your life as a vehicle for change in the world, and you have a greater connection to managing social relationships. Cultural Intelligence is also critical when on the path to seeking clarity of purpose and passion. When you immerse yourself in other cultures, you have a greater appreciation for the life you have and a greater understanding of the importance of embracing all of life's experiences, whether good or bad, and you can use the experiences as a means to contribute to the betterment of humankind!

The confirmation and validation of my purpose and passion was evident when I was selected as a Fulbright Scholar last year through the Bureau of Educational and Cultural Affairs, State Department, Washington, DC, as a result of my international contributions. I'm honored to join the Fulbright ranks of over 250,000 scholars who have made a significant contribution within various countries, as well as the overall goal of advancing mutual understanding among cultures. My purpose and passion was also validated this past year when I worked with one of my former graduates, friend and colleague Dr. Dereje Tessema, to create and chair the International Conference on Interdisciplinary Research Studies, conducted at the George Washington University, Washington DC. The conference is a platform to bring scholars, researchers, policy makers, organizational leaders, academics, and doctoral learners across multiple disciplines together to create and share knowledge regarding trends, best practices, and innovations related to solving complex world issues and challenges. Chairing this conference annually provides an opportunity to impact lives and solve world problems through research.

Dr. Martin Luther King, Jr., said it best when he said, "Everyone cannot be famous, but everyone can be great. Greatness is shown through service." I hope to leave a legacy of greatness through my service contributions. I remember when my late grandfather, Walter D. McCollum, Sr., passed away and the pastor officiating the funeral placed his hands on my shoulder and said to me, "Receive a mantle of great works." I am very clear that my obligation is to continue my grandfather's legacy on a much larger scale. As an extension of his efforts, I am using my ordinary life to impact positive social change in extraordinary ways.

About the Author

Walter Ray McCollum, PhD
Fulbright Scholar

Dr. Walter McCollum is an educator and international consultant. He has been employed by top companies, including Lucent Technologies, Booz Allen & Hamilton, Lockheed Martin, Science Application International Corporation (SAIC), Capgemini, and Sodexo.

Prior to working in the private sector, Dr. McCollum, a Desert Storm veteran, served 13 years in the U.S. Air Force, where he held various Air Force specialties in the areas of information management and communications. His military awards and medals include Air Force Commendation Medal w/1 Oak Leaf Cluster, Joint Meritorious Service Medal, Air Force Achievement Medal w/2 Oak Leaf Clusters, Southwest Asia Service Medal, Humanitarian Service Medal, National Defense Service Medal, Distinguished Graduate Noncommissioned Officer's Academy, Military Citizenship Award Noncommissioned Officer's Academy, and Office of the Secretary of Defense Junior Enlisted Member of the Year.

As a scholar-practitioner, Dr. McCollum has authored and published six books: *Process Improvement in Quality Management Systems: Case Studies Analyzing Carnegie Mellon's Capability Maturity Model*; *Applied Change Management: Approaches to Organizational Change and Transformation*; *Strength of a Black Man: Destined for Self-Empowerment*; *Breakthrough Mentoring in the 21st Century: A Compilation of Life-Altering Experiences*; *How to Use Emotional, Cultural, and Spiritual Intelligence to Mentor Doctoral Learners*; and *Purpose, Hope, and Determination: Transitioning from Ordinary to Extraordinary*. He is also published in several peer-reviewed journals.

Dr. McCollum has also been a professor at several universities, including New York University, Walden University, Northcentral University, Capella University, Upper Iowa University, Argosy University, University of Phoenix, University of the District of Columbia, Central Michigan University, and Colorado State University—Global. He holds a PhD in applied management and decision sciences with a specialization in leadership and organizational change from Walden University, an MA in management from Webster University, a BS in psychology from the State University of New York, Albany, and an AAS in business management from Dabney S. Lancaster Community College.

www.ingramcontent.com/pod-product-compliance
Lightning Source LLC
Chambersburg PA
CBHW060117170426
43198CB00010B/928